HOW TO **PLAY PIANO** AND READ MUSIC

Easy Way to Learn Piano and Sight Read

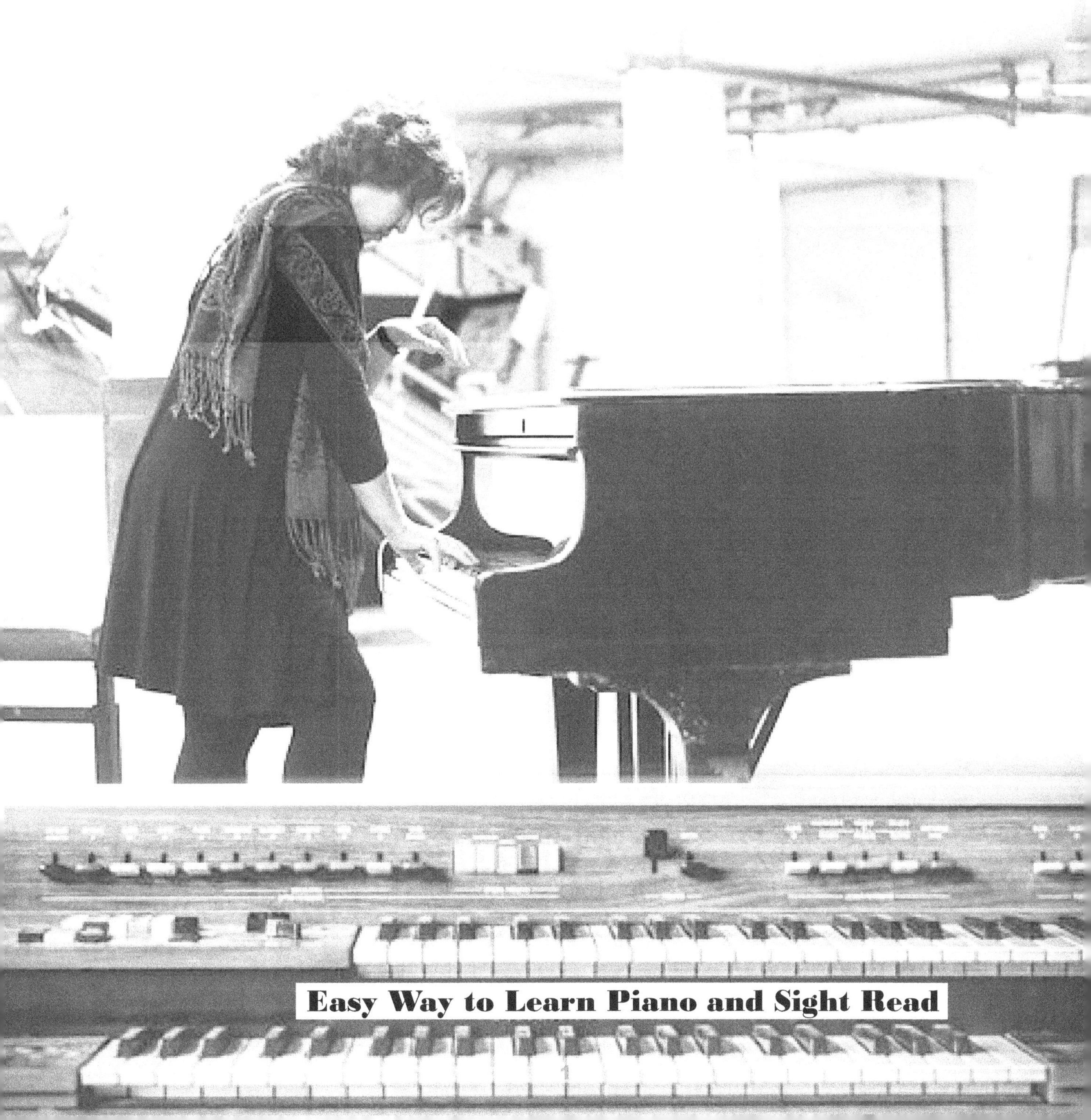

HOW TO PLAY PIANO AND READ MUSIC
Is an
Easy Way to Learn Piano and Sight Read

Copyright © 2018 by Ezra Nwachukwu

Designed and Published by:
EZRA CREATIVE PRODUCTIONS

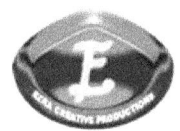

For further information, please contact:

Telephone: +2348109845736

Email: EzraCreativeProductions@gmail.com

Website: EzraCreativeProductions.com

ISBN 978-1-387-55338-9
Lulu.com

CONTENTS

CONTENTS

WHAT IS MUSIC

Music is the combination of sounds in a manner that is pleasant to the ear or agreeable to the ear.

* Also Music is an Organized sound.

For young kids and babes music could be singing, dancing, jumping, clapping... Music is play to them, but that can be seen as attribute and features of music, without sound there's no music because music is made up of sounds.

There're two major kinds of sound: Musical sound and Noise sound. If the sound is arranged in a regular frequency, then it is a musical sound because it's organized.

But if a sound is not arranged and organized, it is a distracting noise.

MUSICAL NOTES
Musical notes are the first seven letters in the English Alphabet:

A, B, C, D, E, F, G.
They are used in naming the Piano Keys.

COMMON SYMBOLS AND MEANING IN MUSIC

Symbol	Meaning
#	Sharp
♭	Flat
♮	Natural

OCTAVE
An Octave is an eight; from Lower key **C to higher** key **C is an octave**, from doh to a higher doh is an Octave

GROUP NAME OF PIANO KEYS

WHAT IS A KEY

A key is a note in which a musical piece is centered around.
We have TWELVE (12) KEYS in music, and on all musical instrument.

The **12 keys** in music are:

<u>A</u>,   <u>A# or Bb</u>,   <u>B</u>,   <u>C</u>,   <u>C# or Db</u>,   <u>D</u>,   <u>D# or Eb</u>,
<u>E</u>,   <u>F</u>,   <u>F# or Gb</u>,   <u>G</u>,   <u>G# or Ab</u>.

IDENTIFICATION OF KEYS ON THE KEYBOARD

(The Piano keys are arranged in Twos and Threes,)

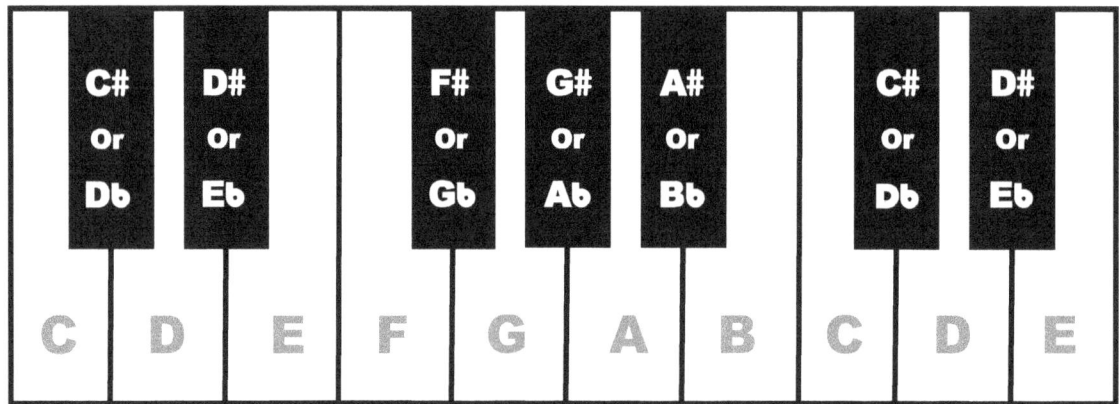

The White keys are called the **Natural Keys**, while the Black keys
are called **Accidental keys** because they possess two names
(Sharp or Flat) which is derived from the white keys.

TONIC SOL - FA

Tonic Solfa are the sol-fas of the Musical note which is:
d, r, m, f, s, l, t, d.

They are equally referred to as the Major Scale, known as
Solmization by the British and Solfagio by the Italian.

TONIC SOL - FA

HOW TO PLAY TONIC SOL - FA (MAJOR SCALE)

From $\overset{1}{d}$ to $\overset{3}{r}$ you leave a note   "FULL TONE"

From $\overset{1}{r}$ to $\overset{3}{m}$ you leave a note   "FULL TONE"

$\overset{1}{m}$ and $\overset{2}{f}$ are together   "SEMI TONE"

From $\overset{1}{f}$ to $\overset{3}{s}$ you leave a note   "FULL TONE"

From $\overset{1}{s}$ to $\overset{3}{l}$ you leave a note   "FULL TONE"

From $\overset{1}{l}$ to $\overset{3}{t}$ you leave a note   "FULL TONE"

$\overset{1}{t}$ and $\overset{2}{d}$ are together   "SEMI TONE"

FINGER NUMBERING

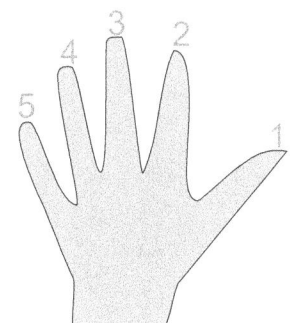
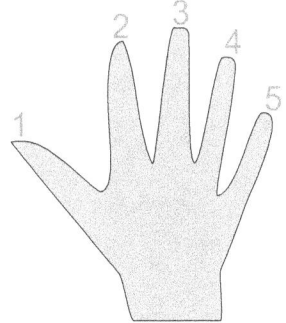

EXERCISE ON LEFT AND RIGHT HAND

<u>LEFT HAND</u>

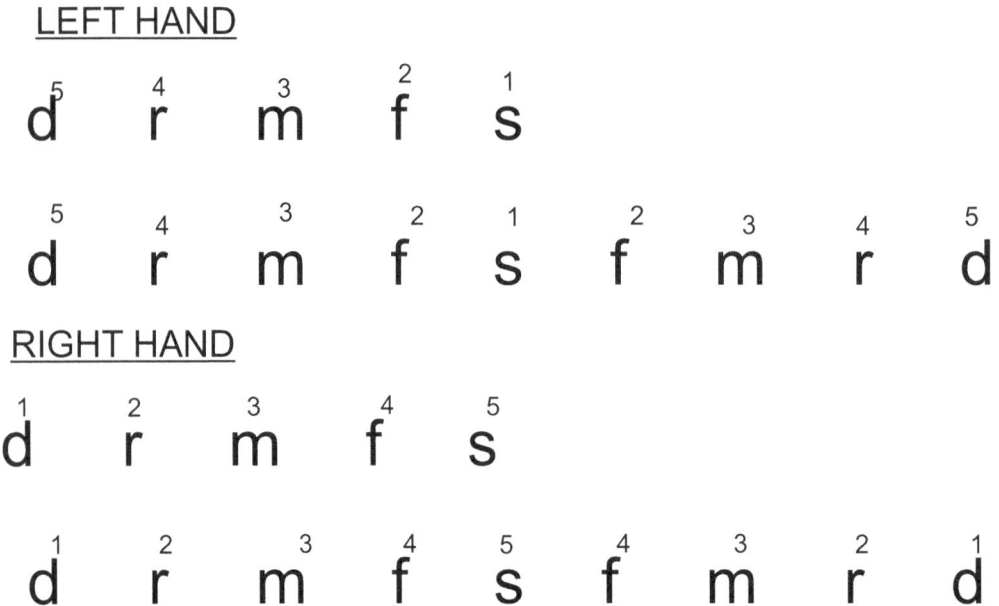

<u>RIGHT HAND</u>

Play each exercise many time one hand after the other,
if you've mastered them, Play it on both hands slowly and gradually
increase your speedand remember to always practice them
among others as it helps to increase your speed.

PROPER FINGERING OF MAJOR SCALE

Right Hand on Key: C, D, E, G, A, B

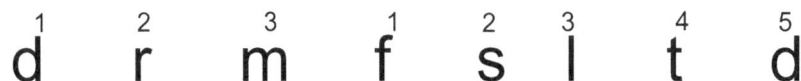

To play it on more than one octave, change your finger after ti
and use the finger you used for the initial doh and continue.
<u>Example:</u>

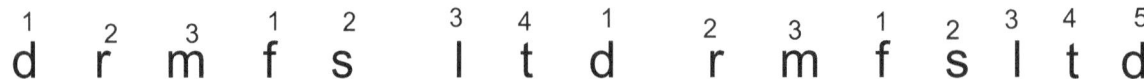

The numbers above the Sol-fa signifies the finger to play it with.

* Practice the scale in ascending order, afterward in desciding order.
After you've played it long enough practice it in both ascending and descending order.

PROPER FINGERING OF MAJOR SCALE

Right Hand on Key: C#

^{2}	^{3}	^{1}	^{2}	^{3}	^{4}	^{1}	^{2}
d	r	m	f	s	l	t	d

Right Hand on Key: E♭

^{3}	^{1}	^{2}	^{3}	^{4}	^{1}	^{2}	^{3}
d	r	m	f	s	l	t	d

Right Hand on Key: F

^{1}	^{2}	^{3}	^{4}	^{1}	^{2}	^{3}	^{4}
d	r	m	f	s	l	t	d

Right Hand on Key: F#

^{2}	^{3}	^{4}	^{1}	^{2}	^{3}	^{1}	^{2}
d	r	m	f	s	l	t	d

Right Hand on Key: A♭

^{3}	^{4}	^{1}	^{2}	^{3}	^{1}	^{2}	^{3}
d	r	m	f	s	l	t	d

Right Hand on Key: B♭

^{4}	^{1}	^{2}	^{3}	^{1}	^{2}	^{3}	^{4}
d	r	m	f	s	l	t	d

* Please practice the scale in both ascending and descending order
  till you know it well enough, then move on to other Lessons.

PROPER FINGERING OF MAJOR SCALE

Left Hand on Key: C, D, E, F, G, A

5	4	3	2	1	3	2	1
d	r	m	f	s	l	t	d

In other to run it on more than one Octave, change your finger after doh and use the finger you used while playing re. (Finger 4)
Example:

5	4	3	2	1	3	2	1	4	3	2	1	3	2	1
d	r	m	f	s	l	t	d	r	m	f	s	l	t	d

Left Hand on Key: C#, E♭, A♭, B♭

3	2	1	4	3	2	1	3
d	r	m	f	s	l	t	d

Left Hand on Key: F#

4	3	2	1	3	2	1	4
d	r	m	f	s	l	t	d

Left Hand on Key: B

4	3	2	1	4	3	2	1
d	r	m	f	s	l	t	d

To play it on more than one octave, Start with the finger you are to end with, Example:

1	3	2	1	4	3	2	1	3	2	1	4	3	2	1
d	r	m	f	s	l	t	d	r	m	f	s	l	t	d

* Please practice the Lesson again and again, afterwards play it on both hands.

TONIC SOL - FA READING

Half beat   Full beat (1)   Two beat   Three beat   Four beat

d .   r :   m :-   F:-:   S:-:-

Six beat

L:-:-:-

SIGN		MEANING
.	-------------------	half seconds
:	-------------------	one seconds
: .	-------------------	one and half seconds
: -	-------------------	two secOnds
: - :	-------------------	three seconds
: - : -	-------------------	four seconds
: - : - : -	-------------------	six seconds

MELODY

Is a sequence of sol-fa notes that makes up a musical phrase

ELSHADDAI SOL-FA NOTE (MELODY)

r : m: f : -
f : m: r : -
s : f : m : -
f . m: r :   d : -
r : m: f : -
m . r : d :   r : -
m : r : d : -   r : - m : -
r : m: f : -   f : m: r : -
s : f : m : -   f . m: r : d : -
r : m: f : -   m . r :   d :   r : -
d : t : d : - : -

SONG RYLICS

Elshaddai elshaddai elohim and Adonai age to age you're still the same; by the power of your name, Elshaddai elshaddai elohim and Adonai i will praise and lift you high Elshaddai.

HARMONY (CHORD)

Is the simultaneous relationship of notes in a vertical order.

Example:
A fifth Chord added an octave in arpeggio style.
d : s : d,   f : d : f,   l : m : l,   s : r : s...
It enriches melodies.

CHORDS

Chord is the combination of two, three or more notes
.
When two, three or more note is being played at the same time.
It harmonizes melodic sounds.

There are two main kind of chords; MAJOR and MINOR CHORD.

MAJOR CHORDS

On any key once you've gotten your Tonic sol-fa notes,

combine: **d   m   s** ➡ it becomes a MAJOR CHORD (Triad)

PRACTICAL EXAMPLE OF YOUR MAJOR CHORD

When played on C, it's called a C Major Chord: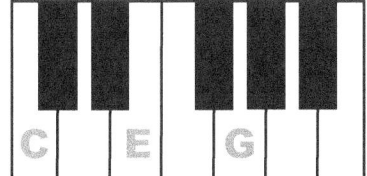

When played on C#, it's called a C# Major Chord: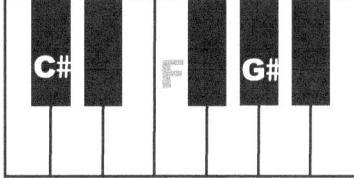

When played on D, it's called a D Major Chord: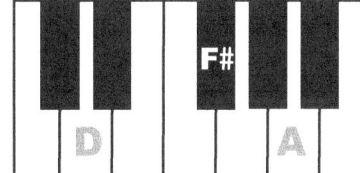

When played on E♭, it's called a E♭ Major Chord: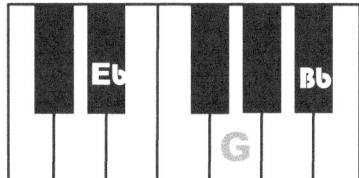

When played on E, it's called a E Major Chord: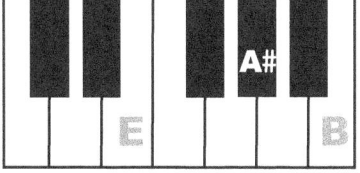

When played on F, it's called a F Major Chord: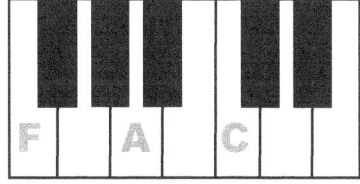

MAJOR CHORDS

PRACTICAL EXAMPLE OF YOUR MAJOR CHORD

When played on F# it's called: F# Major Chord:

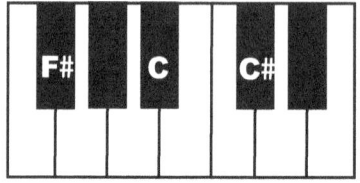

When played on G it's called a G Major Chord:

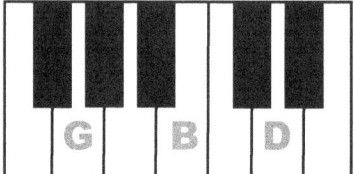

When played on A♭ it's called; A♭ Major Chord:

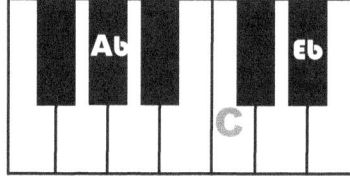

When played on A it's called; A Major Chord:

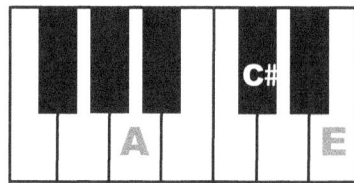

On B♭ it's called a; B♭ Major Chord:

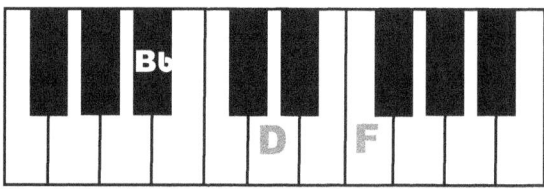

On B it's called a; B Major Chord:

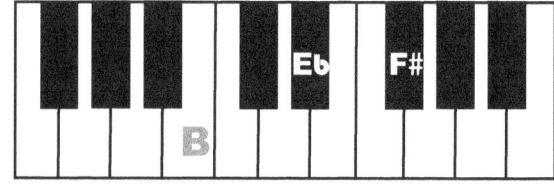

When you flat the middle note of your major chord in root position, it becomes a MINOR CHORD: **d mo s**

CHORD EXERCISE ON LEFT AND RIGHT HAND

RIGHT HAND

¹d	³m	⁵s	

$$\overset{1}{d} \quad \overset{3}{m} \quad \overset{5}{s}$$

$$\overset{5}{s} \quad \overset{3}{m} \quad \overset{1}{d}$$

$$\overset{1}{d} \quad \overset{3}{m} \quad \overset{5}{s} \quad \overset{3}{m}$$

$$\overset{5}{s} \quad \overset{3}{m} \quad \overset{1}{d} \quad \overset{3}{m}$$

LEFT HAND

$$\overset{5}{d} \quad \overset{3}{m} \quad \overset{1}{s}$$

$$\overset{1}{s} \quad \overset{3}{m} \quad \overset{5}{d}$$

$$\overset{5}{d} \quad \overset{3}{m} \quad \overset{1}{s} \quad \overset{3}{m}$$

$$\overset{1}{s} \quad \overset{3}{m} \quad \overset{5}{d} \quad \overset{3}{m}$$

TONIC NOTATION CHORDS

CHORD NUMBER	SOL-FA NOTES OF CHORD	CHORD TYPE
i Chord	d m s	Major
ii Chord	r f l	Minor
iii Chord	m s t	Minor
iv Chord	f l d	Major
v Chord	s t r	Major
vi Chord	l d m	Minor
vii Chord	t r f	Diminished

PROGRESSION

Progression is the Chord change and movement in a musical piece

BASIC CHORD PROGRESSIONS

i ⟶ **Do Chord**

iv ⟶ **Fa Chord**

v ⟶ **So Chord**

* Roman figures are used to number chords and identify them.

BASIC CHORD PROGRESSION TO SONGS

HOW TO PLAY JEHOVAH YOU ARE THE MOST HIGH

Rylics => Jehovah you are the most high
Chord =>   (i chord) (iv chord) (i chord)

Jehovah you are the most high God
(v chord) (i chord)

CHORDS				SOL-FA NOTES			
i	(d	m	s)	m :	r :	d :	
iv	(f	l	d)	l .	l .	l .	l .
i	(d	m	s)	d :- m :	r :	d :	
v	(s	t	r)	t . t .	t :	m :	r :
i	(d	m	s)	d :-:-			

HOW TO PLAY OUR GOD IS AWESOME

Rylics => Our God is Awesome he can move Mountains
Chord =>   (i chord) (i chord) (v chord)

Rylics => Keep me in the valley Hide me from the rain
Chord =>   (vi chord) (iv chord)

www.EzraCreativeProductions.com   In a World of Creation Where Ideas Come to Life...

17

HOW TO PLAY OUR GOD IS AWESOME

Rylics =>   Our God is Awesome he heals me when am broken

Chord =>   (i chord)   (i chord)   (v chord)

Rylics =>   Strenghten where am Weaken Forever he will reign

Chord =>   (vi chord)   (iv chord)

CHORDS	SOL-FA NOTES
	m : r : s:
i (d m s)	d : d : d . r . m :
v (s t r)	r : r : r . m . f :
vi (l d m)	m : m : m . r . d . t . d .
iv (f l d)	l :-: Da Ca po.

Da Ca-po (D.C) - means; Go back to begining and play it again.

Da Ca-po Al fine - means; Go back to begining and finish at the word fine.

HOW TO PLAY AM TRADING MY SORROW

Rylics =>   Am Trading my Sor   row   Am trading my   Pa - in

Chord =>   (i chord)   (iv chord)   (vi chord)   (v chord)   (i chord) (iv chord)   (vi chord) (v chord)

Rylics =>   Am Letting them go   for the Joy of the L o r d   ~

Chord =>   (i chord) (iv chord)   (vi chord)   (v chord)   (i chord)   (iv chord) (vi chord) (v chord)

CHORD PROGRESSION OF AM TRADING MY SORROW

* Try pouncing (i) and (iv) Chord twice.

CHORDS

i   (d   m   s)

iv   (f   l   d)

vi   (l   d   m)

v   (s   t   r)

CHORD PROGRESSION OF I NEED AN ANGEL

Rylics =>   I   need   an An - gel   I'm cal - ling an An - gel
Chord => (i chord) (vi chord)   (iv chord) (v chord)   (i chord) (vi chord) (iv chord) (v chord)

Rylics =>   Send   me an An - gel   God
Chord =>   (i chord) (vi chord)   (iv chord) (v chord)   (Vi chord)

CHORDS   SOL-FA NOTES

i   (d   m   s)   s   :

vi   (l   d   m)   m   :
                                                    Three Times
iv   (f   l   d)   d . d .

v   (s   t   r)   r   :

iv   (f   l   d)   d   :-:-   Da Capo

www.EzraCreativeProductions.com   In a World of Creation Where Ideas Come to Life...

19

CHORD POSITIONS AND INVERSION

Chord	Root Position			1st Inversion			2nd Inversion			Chord Type
I	d	m	s	m	s	d	s	d	m	Major
Ii	r	f	l	f	l	r	l	r	f	Minor
iii	m	s	t	s	t	m	t	m	s	Minor
Iv	f	l	d	l	d	f	d	f	l	Major
V	s	t	r	t	r	s	r	s	t	Major
Vi	l	d	m	d	m	l	m	l	d	Minor
vii	t	r	f	r	f	t	f	t	r	Diminished

PERFECT CADENCE is a chord progression that goes from V - i

PLAGAL CADENCE is a chord progression that goes from ii - i, or from iv - i (also know as AMEN CADENCE)

* Go through the lessons again and make sure you've mastered them and move on to the next lesson.

CHORD PROGRESSION WITH INVERSIONS

By now you must have learnt some simple songs!, We'll be going through some songs using the inversions that we've learnt.

HOW TO PLAY JEHOVAH YOU ARE THE MOST HIGH (with Chord Inversions)

CHORDS	POSITION
i (d m s)	**Root Position**
iv (d f l)	**2nd Inversion**
i (d m s)	**Root Position**
v (t r s)	**1st Inversion**

HOW TO PLAY OPEN THE FLOOD GATE OF HEAVEN

Rylics =>	Open the flood-gate of heaven let it rain let it rain			
Chord =>	(i chord)	(v chord)	(vi chord)	(iv chord)

CHORDS	POSITION
i (d m s)	**Root Position**
v (t r s)	**1st Inversion**
vi (d m l)	**1st Inversion**
iv (d f l)	**2nd Inversion**

HOW TO PLAY ELSHADDAI WITH CHORD

CHORDS				POSITION
i	(d	m	s)	Root Position
iv	(d	f	l)	2nd Inversion
v	(t	r	s)	1st Inversion
iii	(t	m	s)	2nd Inversion
i	(d	m	s)	Root Position
iv	(d	f	l)	2nd Inversion
v	(t	r	s)	1st Inversion
i	(d	m	s)	Root Position

HOW TO PLAY ELSHADDAI

Rylics =>   Elsha ddai elsha ddai Elo him and Adonai
Chord =>   (i chord)   (iv chord)   (v chord)   (iii chord)   (i chord)

Rylics =>   I'll Praise and lift you High   Elshaddai
Chord =>   (iv chord)   (v chord)   (i chord)

HOW TO PLAY BOWDOWN AND WORSHIP HIM

Rylics =>	Bowdown and Wor		ship	him
Chord =>	(vi chord)		(vi chord) (vii chord)	(i chord)

Rylics =>	Bowdown and Wor		ship	him
Chord =>	(vi chord)		(vi chord) (vii chord)	(i chord)

Rylics =>	Wor ship	him	O worship him
Chord =>	(iv chord) (vi chord)	(v chord)	(iv chord)

CHORDS	POSITION
vi (l d m)	Root Position
vii (t r f)	Root Position
i (d m s)	Root Position
vi (l d m)	Root Position
vii (t r f)	Root Position
i (d m s)	Root Position
iv (d f l)	2nd Inversion
Vi (d m l)	1st Inversion
V (t r s)	1st Inversion
iv (d f l)	2nd Inversion

NICE CHORD SUBSTITUTES FOR MAJOR CHORD TRIAD

NINTH CHORD (9th)	SUSPENDED SECOND (sus 2)
d r m s	d r s

PERFECT THIRD (3rd)	SUSPENDED FOURTH (sus 4)
d m	d f s

PERFECT FIFTH (5fth)	OCTAVE (8th)
d s	d d

SIXTH (6th)	MAJOR SEVENTH (M7)
d m s l	d m s t

SIXTH ADDED NINTH (6TH, 9TH)	MINOR SEVENTH (m7)
d r m s l	d m s ta

POLYCHORD

Polychord is when you simultaneously play one chord over another
(two different), Example on Key C is: doh chord over La chord (C / A chord)

<u>LEFT HAND</u>	<u>RIGHT HAND</u>
l d m	d m s
m s t	s t r
f l d	l d m

*Try playing the new chords that have been introduced one hand after the other and
listen deeply to the sound been heard,

then afterwards try out both hands and listen again to the sounds, try to distinguish it
from the other.
(It's not compulsory to perfectly tell the sounds at this stage but it is encouraged to try)

COMBINATION OF CHORDS

CHORDS	LEFT HAND--"Perfect 5fth"		RIGHT HAND- Suspended 2nd			
I	d	s	d	r	s	
Iv	f	d	f	s	d	
Vi	l	m	l	d	m	- (Minor)
V	S	r	s	l	r	
Iv	f	d	f	s	d	
Vi	l	m	l	t	m	
V	S	r	s	l	r	
Iv	f	d	f	s	d	

*Play the chords combination on different timing all over again, afterwards play your right hand notes simultaneously, one after the other (in Arpeggio style) as you strike your lefthand chord

ARPEGGIO STYLE

Arpeggio style is when you play the notes of your chords successively while holding the previous note down in a vertical order. Example:

d - m - s - d
f - l - d - f

www.EzraCreativeProductions.com   In a World of Creation Where Ideas Come to Life...

25

COMBINATION OF CHORDS

d_I - d^I

Higher Octave doh

Lower Octave doh

When you see a I figure down after a sol-fa note it means you are to: play a Lower octave doh, If you see the I figure up after the sol-fa note it means: Play a Higher doh.

HOW TO USE OCTAVE ADDED FIFTH IN ARPEGGIO STYLE

ELSHADDAI ELSHADDAI

Harmony (Arpeggio)		Melody (Arpeggio)
d m s	⟷	
	⟷	r : m :
f : d : f	⟷	f : - f : m :
s : r : s	⟷	r : - s : f :
m : t : m	⟷	m : - f . m : r :
d : s : d	⟷	d : - r : m :
f : d : f	⟷	f : - m . r : d :
s : r : s	⟷	r : - m : r :
d : s : d	⟷	d : -

ADVANCE SIGHT READING OF SOL-FA NOTES USING SATB

Acronym		Meaning
S/T	⟷	Suprano (Treble)
A	⟷	Auto
T	⟷	Tenor
B	⟷	Bass

I WILL DO MY BEST

S/T	m : m : r : r :	d : d : t : t :	l . l . l . l . t : s :	d :-:- Fine
A	s : s : d : d:	l : l : se : s :	f . f . f . f . s : s :	s :-:-
T	m : m : s : s:	m : m : m : m :	d . d . d . d . r : f :	m :-:-
B	d : d : s : s :	l : l : m : m :	f . f . f . f . s : s :	d :-:-

I will do my best for Jesus,   Sing unto the Lord my soul. : - : -

S/T	s : s : f : f :	m : m : r : r :	s : s : f : f :	r : fe : s :-
A	d : d : d : d:	d : d : t : t :	d : d : l : l :	fe : l : t :-
T	m : m : s : s:	l : l : l : l :	m : m : d : d:	r : r : r : m :
B	d : d : l : l :	d : d : s : s :	d : d : f : f :	l : r : s :-

D . C al fine

I will praise him with my whole heart, I will worship Christ my King. :-:-

STAFF / STAVE

Stave is a Musical diagram used for writing notations.
It consist of <u>Five lines and Four spaces.</u>

A Clef is a Musical symbol used to indicate the pitch range of written notes.

Basically there are two type of Clef, the Bass and Treble Clef.

BASS CLEF (also known as F CLEF)

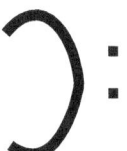

TREBLE CLEF (also known as G CLEF)

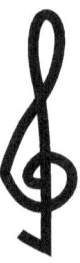

They are placed at the beginning of a stave to show the octave in which the notes are to be played from.

LINES AND SPACES ON STAVE

NAME OF SPACES ON TREBLE STAVE

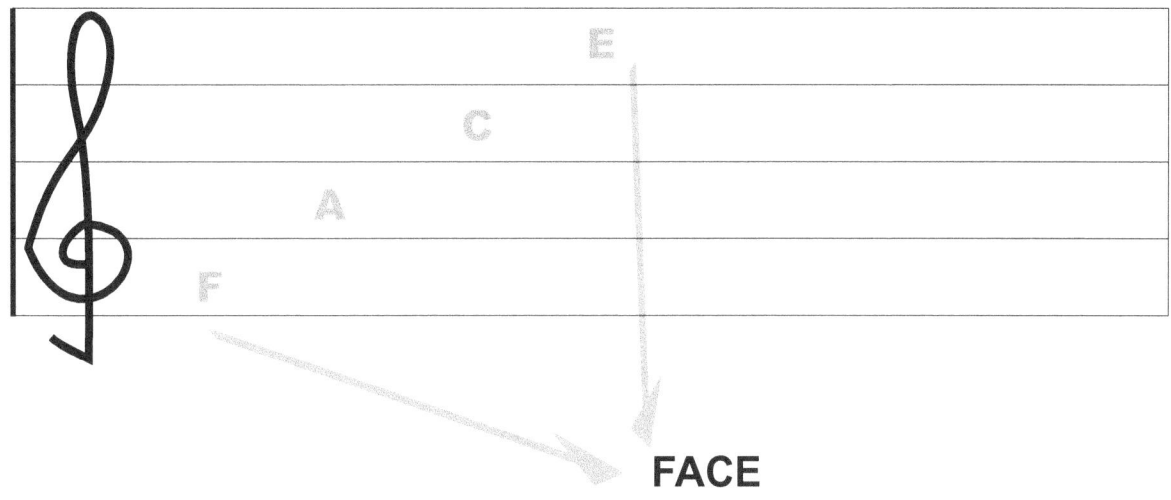

FACE

NAME OF LINES ON TREBLE STAVE

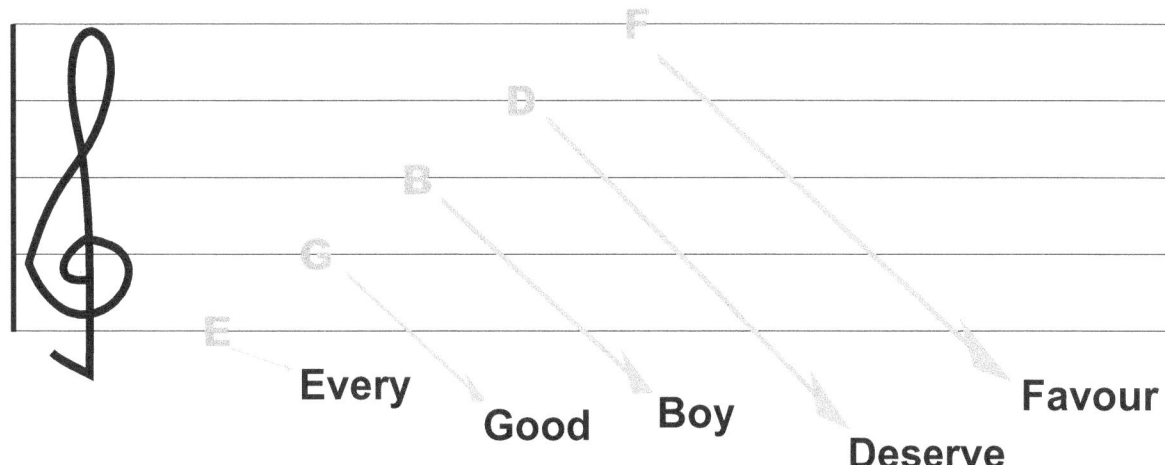

Every Good Boy Deserve Favour

LINES AND SPACES ON STAVE

NAME OF SPACES ON BASS STAVE

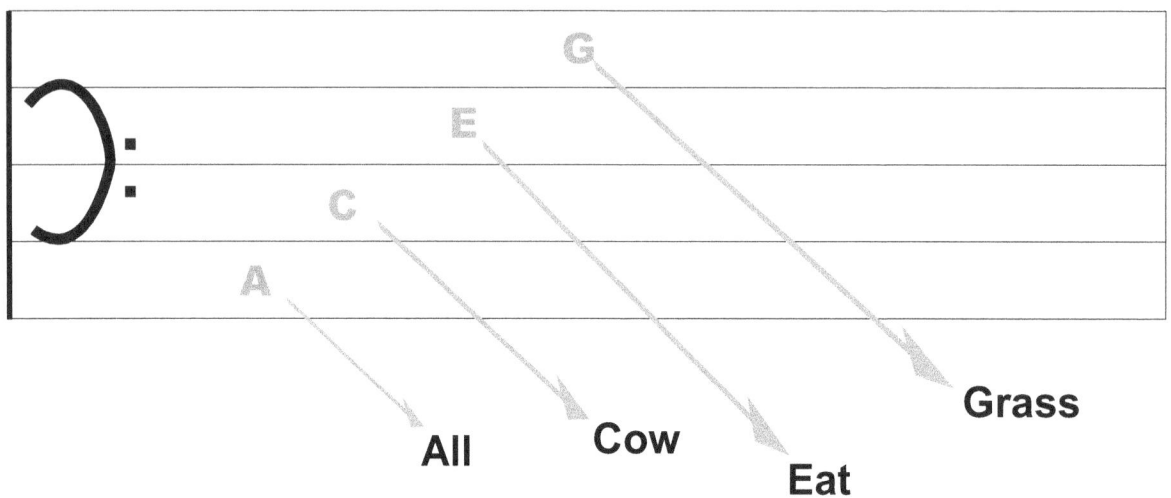

NAME OF LINES ON TREBLE STAVE

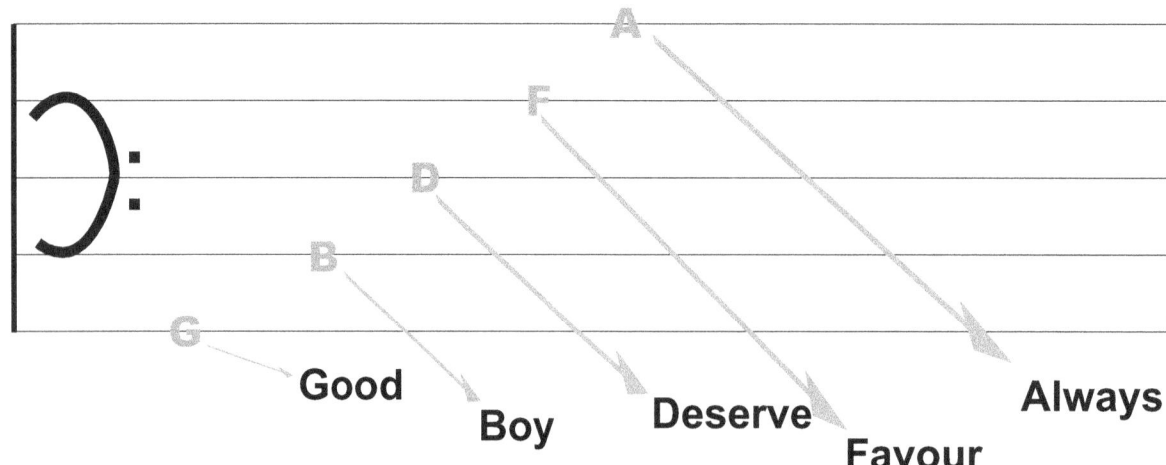

THE GREAT STAVE (also known as the GRAND STAVE)

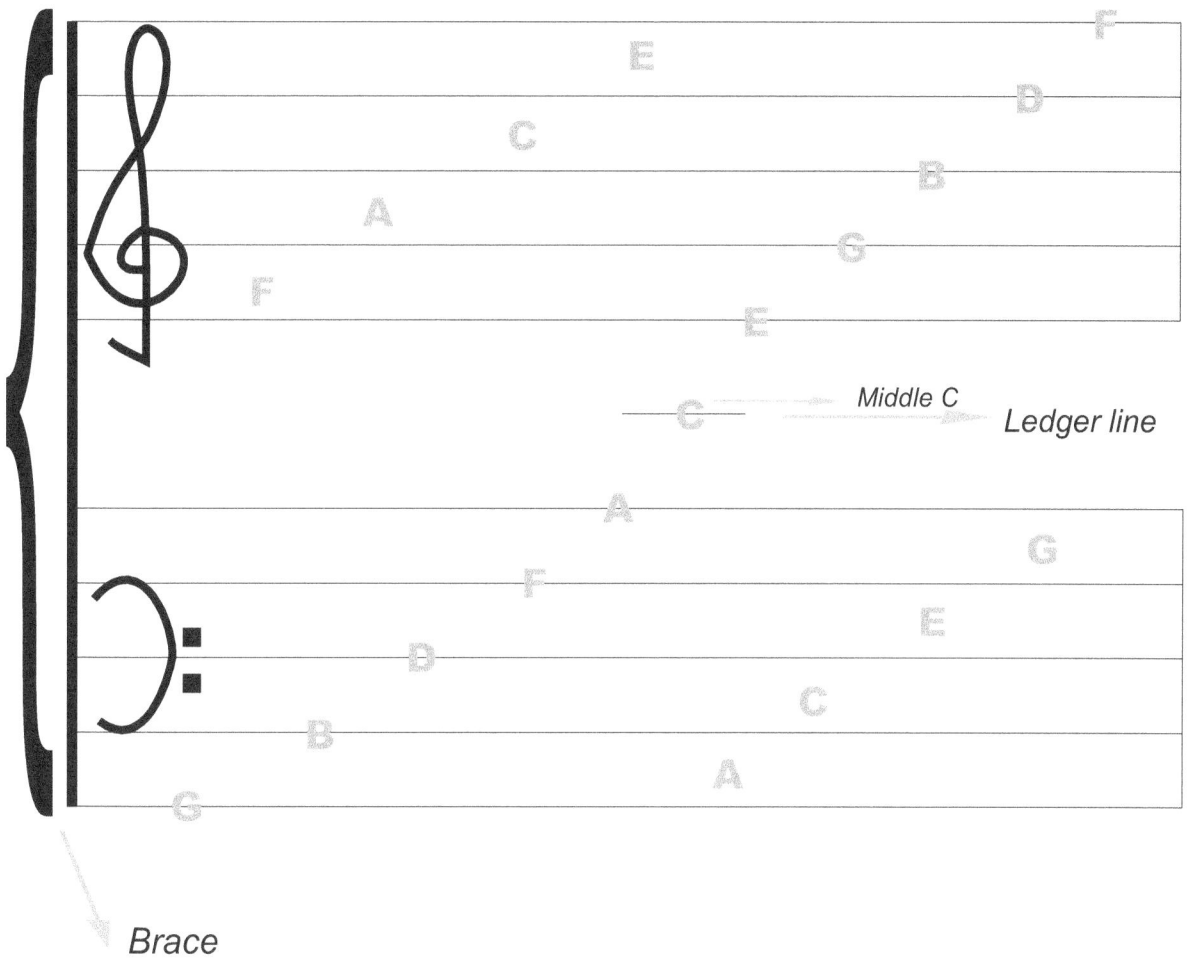

Brace

BRACE: A brace is used to join the Bas**s** and Treble stave or
Multiple staves that represent single instrument such as
(Piano, Organ)

LEDGER LINE: Ledger line is used to extend the stave to pitches
 above or below the stave.

 Multiple Ledger lines can be used
 when necessary to notate pitches even farther above or below the
stave.

BAR LINES AND MEASURE

MEASURES are groupings of notes usually grouped in Meter

METER is a portion or segment in a musical piece.

BAR Lines are used to separate a musical line into Measures.
Bar lines shows us where one Meter ends and another begins.

Single bar line tell us where the measures are, Double bar lines in between the musical line signifies a Major change in the music, such as a new musical section or a new time Signature.

Double bar line at the end of a musical line tells us that the piece of Music is over.

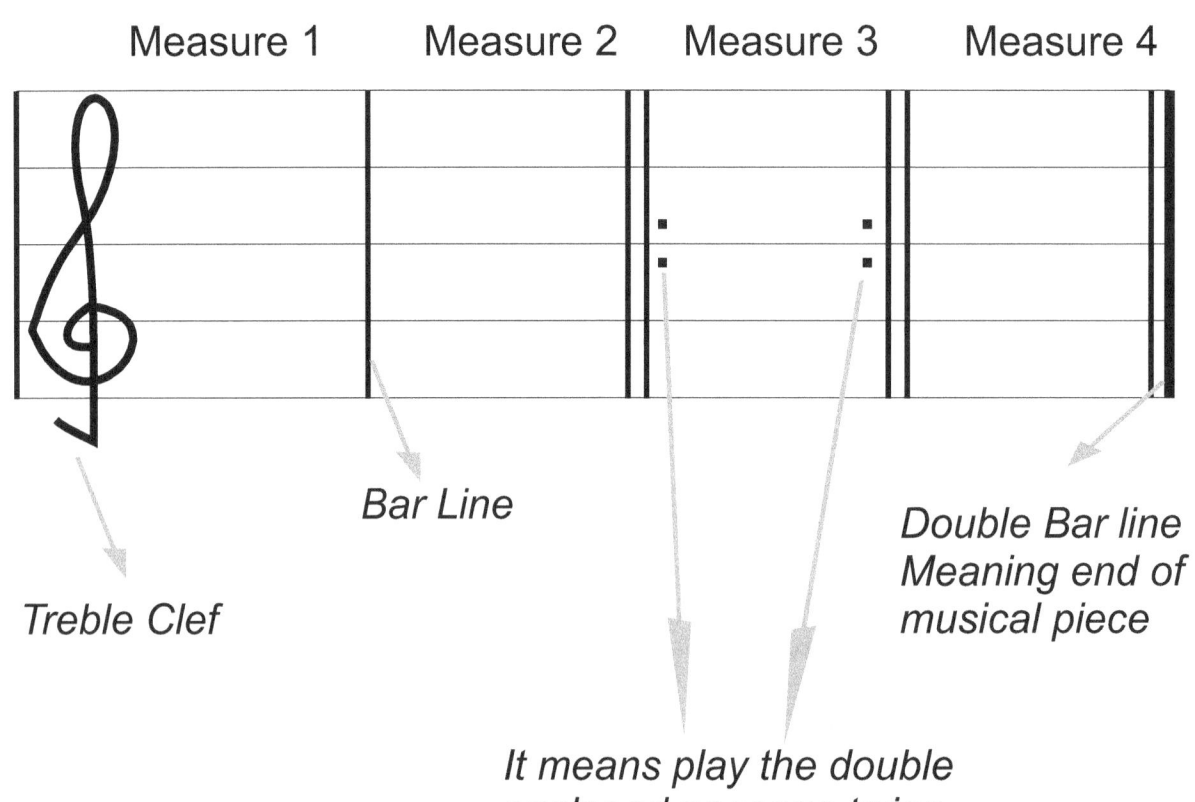

Measure 1   Measure 2   Measure 3   Measure 4

Bar Line

Treble Clef

Double Bar line Meaning end of musical piece

It means play the double enclosed passage twice

KEY SIGNATURE

A Key is a note in which musical piece is centered around.

keys are usually represented with the Sharp and Flat symbol;
(#, b) on the Stave, placed after the clef symbol.

Key C is a Neutral Key, it doesn't have any Sharp or flat symbol representing it.

*(Key **C**)*

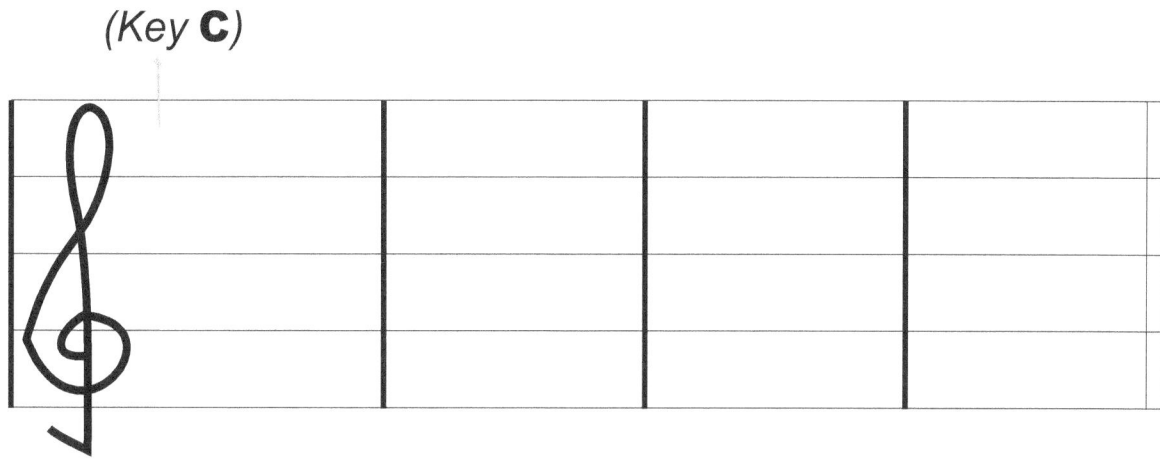

*(Key **D b**)*

It has Five (5) flat symbol after the Clef.

KEY SIGNATURE

(Key **D***)*

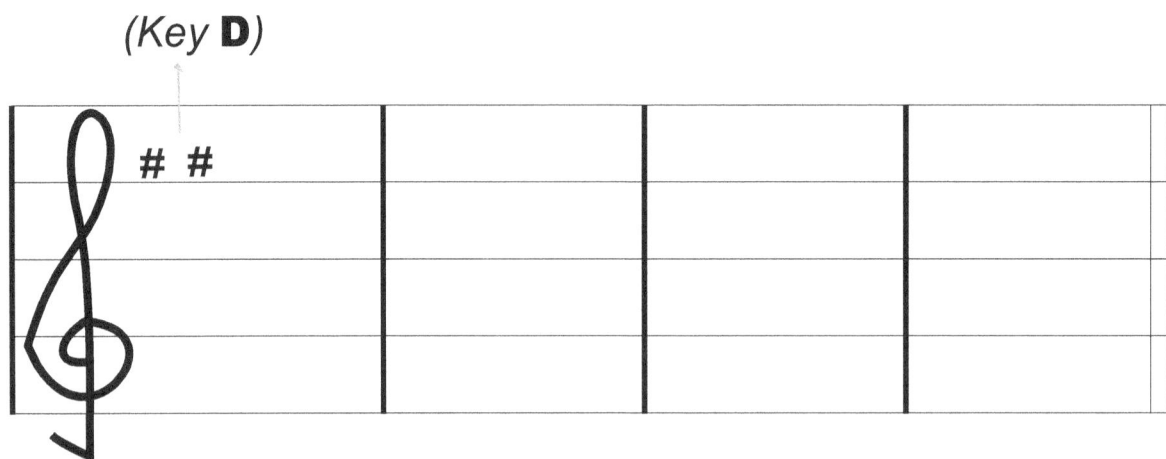

It has Two (2)Sharp symbol after the Clef.

(Key **E♭***)*

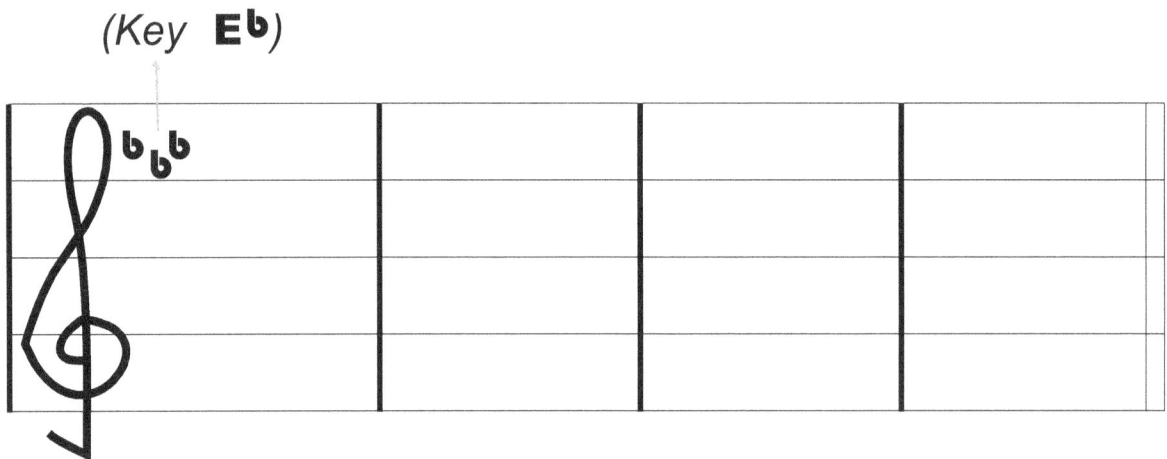

It has Three (3) flat symbol after the Clef.

(Key **E***)*

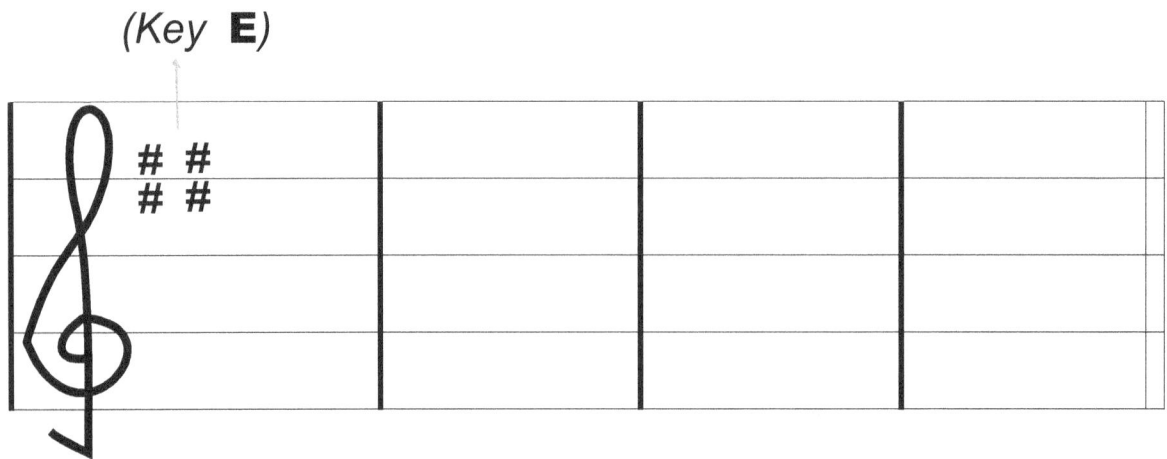

It has Four (4) Sharp symbol after the Clef.

KEY SIGNATURE

(Key **F**)

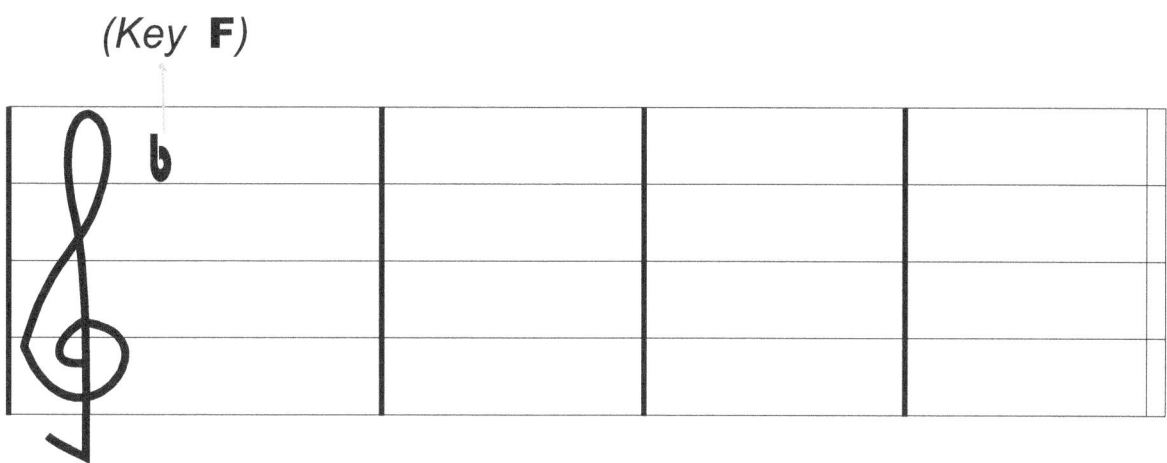

It has One (1) flat symbol after the Clef.

(Key **F#**)

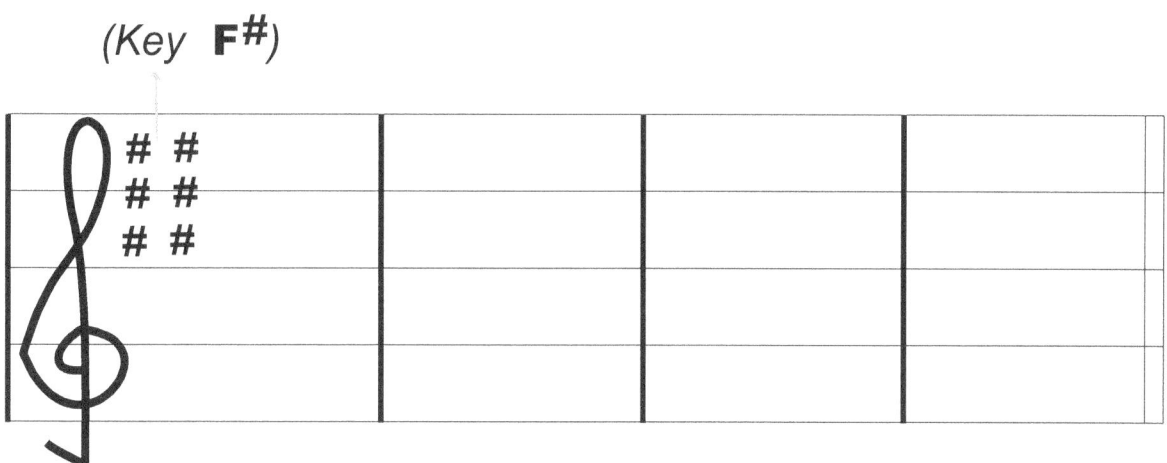

It has Six (6) flat symbol after the Clef.

(Key **G**)

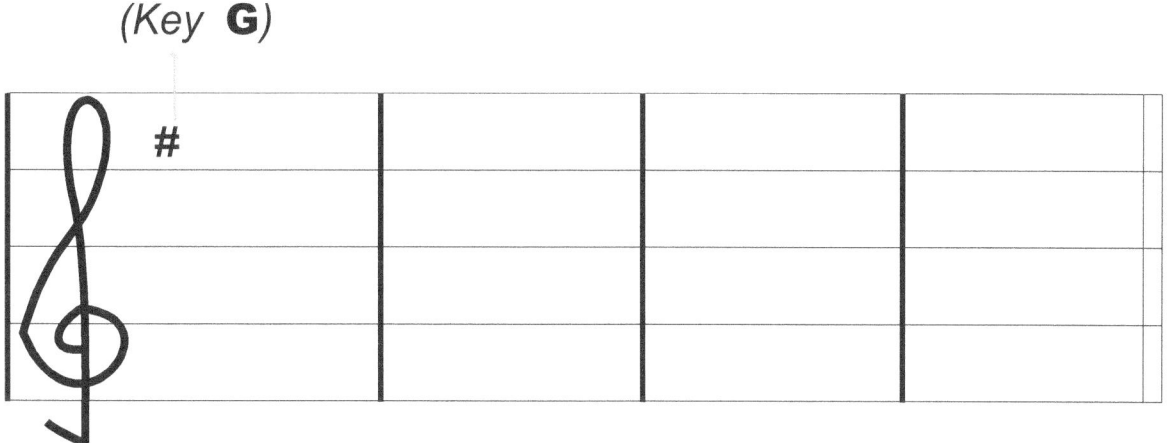

It has One (1) Sharp symbol after the Clef.

KEY SIGNATURE

(Key A♭)

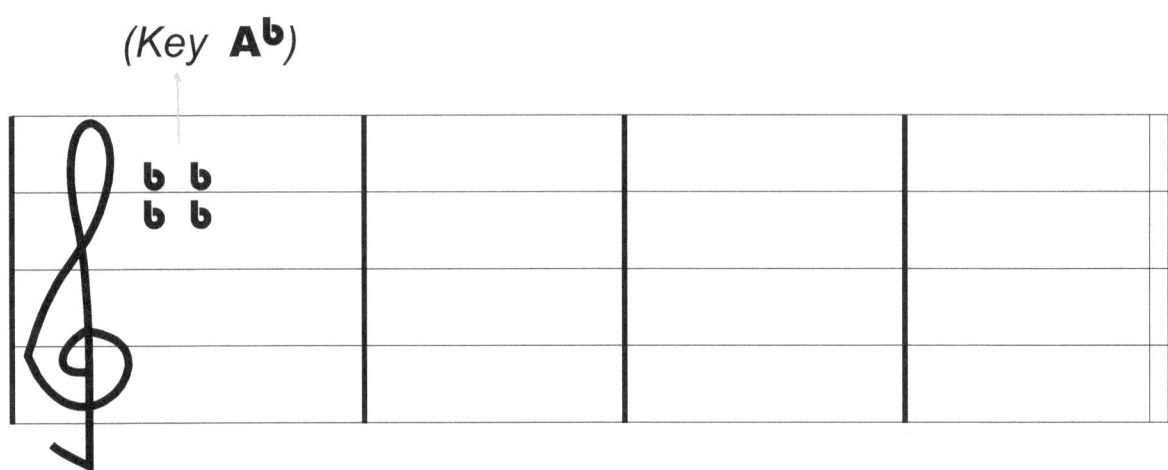

It has Four (4) flat symbol after the Clef.

(Key A)

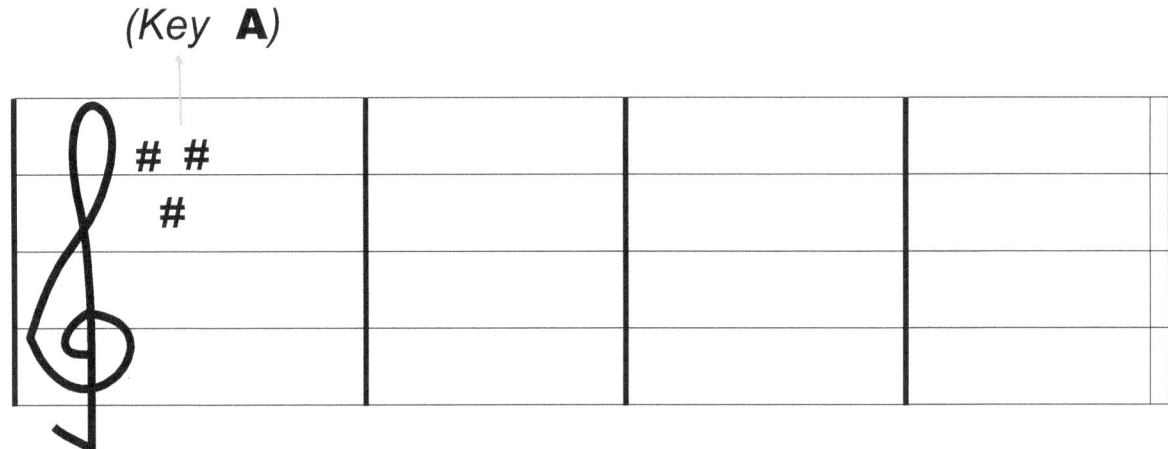

It has Three (3) Sharp symbol after the Clef.

(Key B♭)

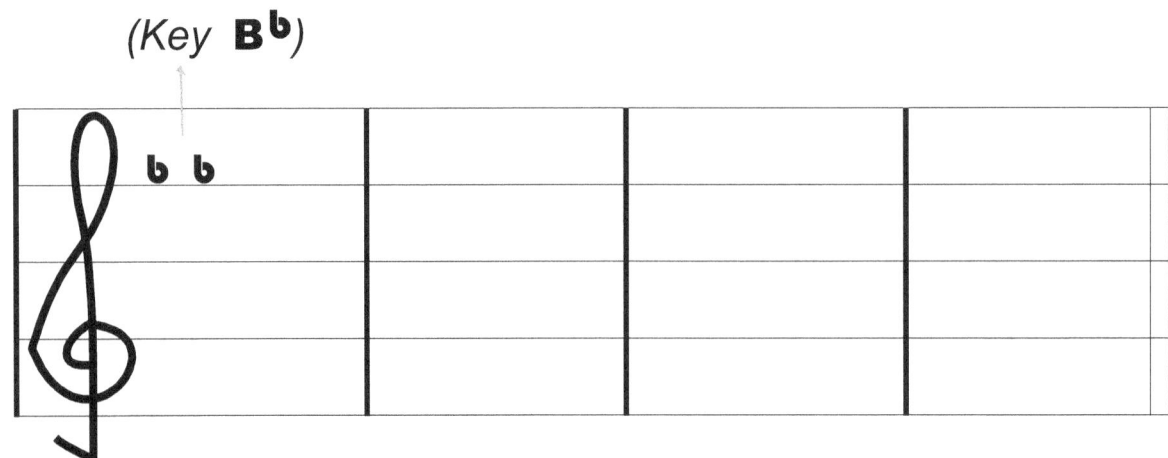

It has Two (2) flat symbol after the Clef.

KEY SIGNATURE

(Key **B***)*

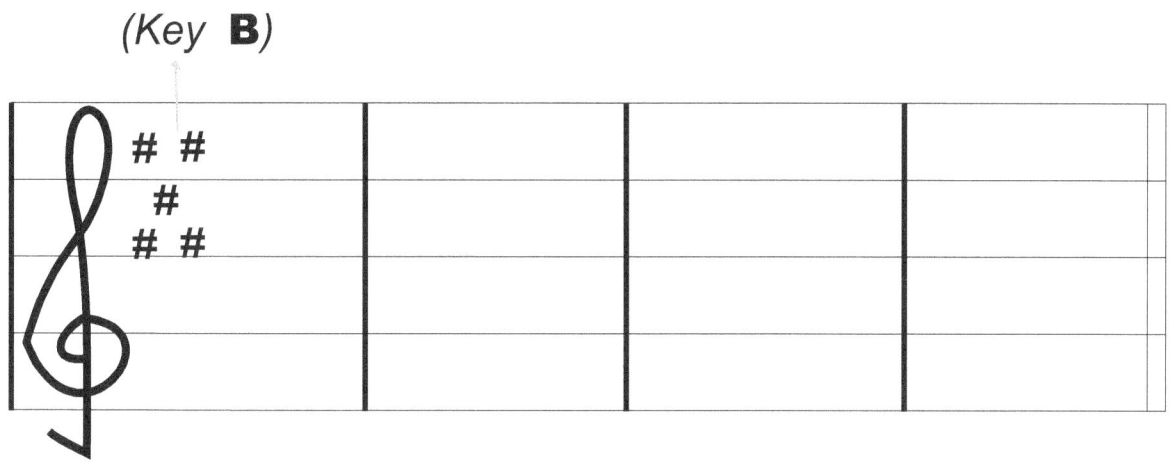

It has Five (5) Sharp symbol after the Clef.

CLEF INDICATIONS FOR SUITABLE OCTAVE

An 8 over a clef means you should play the notes of the clef an Octave higher than the original writing.

A 15 above a clef means you should play the notes of the clef Two Octave higher

An 8 below a clef means you should play the notes of the clef an Octave lower than the original writing.

A 15 below a clef means you should play the notes of the clef Two Octave lower.

KEY SIGNATURE

KEY SIGNATURE		KEY NOTE
♭	⟶	**F** Major
♭ ♭	⟶	**B** Flat
♭ ♭ ♭	⟶	**E** Flat
♭ ♭ ♭ ♭	⟶	**A** Flat
♭ ♭ ♭ ♭ ♭	⟶	**D** Flat
	⟶	**C** Major (It has no sharp or flat sign)
#	⟶	**G** Major
# #	⟶	**D** Major
# # #	⟶	**A** Major
# # # #	⟶	**E** Major
# # # # #	⟶	**B** Major
# # # # # #	⟶	**F** Sharp

GUIDELINE TO SIGHT READING FASTER AND BETTER

28 TIPS TO LEARNING SIGHT READING

1   Create a schedule for practicing each day

2   Learn and memorize key signatures.

3   Master your scale in ascending and descending order.

4   Start with simple sheet music with easy notes and gradually attempt other advance piece with complex note structures

5   Take a minute to Look through the piece you're sight reading. Read through the notes and observe significant changes and where they occur before you play.

6 Take a deep breathe, properly position yourself and relax, When you start playing, keep going even if you make a mistake don't stop, try to play the right note the next time.

7   Pay attention to arrangements, including scales and arpeggio style. If you recognize patterns it will give you enough time to see and understand the piece.

8   Practice beforehand, while the piece is being handed out scrutinize it, study the road map, try and figure out the fingerings with and without a keyboard.

9   Stay focused, keep your eyes on the page your playing and read each note.

10 In other to build your sight reading skill don't memorize any passage, phrase or note.
Immediately you end the piece play a different piece in other to build sight reading skill and not just building your memory muscle!

11 While studying the sheet music you may memorize THE FLOW of the piece to enable you prepare for unfamiliar change and movement, but never cram the notes and don't play from your head!
Be sure to really look and see each note as you play them.

12 Use a Metronome to keep the beat, but in absence of a metronome Tap any of your legs which you're comfortable with to the rhythm and timing of the music.

13   A good book with simple layout, quality construction and large enough stave and notes to read will help a lot.

14 Don't skip lessons when practicing, but you can ignore some difficult signs on the sheet to get the basic movement and flow of the piece first, then latter play it exactly.

GUIDELINE TO SIGHT READING FASTER AND BETTER

28 TIPS TO LEARNING SIGHT READING

15 Familiarize yourself with different rhymes and rhythms.

16 20 minute practice a day will improve your speed to sight reading and make you become used to sight reading. Use a timer or watch to time yourself for a minimum of 20 minute practice a day.

17 Get some computer software for musical training, that can enable you printout the sheet music also, you can search or google online for materials and programs.

18 Play your major and minor scale on the key of the musical piece you're about sight reading.

19 Get book materials with both treble and bass clef, even if your learning only one clef. It's a great advantage to be able to read more than one clef.

20 Concentrate on a single clef as you practice, then afterwards attempt playing both clef.

21 Get books with many easy examples that progresses from simple to advanced lessons, popular and unfamiliar songs too.

22 If you're opportune hear the actual record of the song to get the feel and really understand the music.

23 Practice playing without looking at your hands.

24 Swiftly glide your hands on the piano keys to feel and locate the black keys which are arranged in Two's and Three's, it'll enable you properly position your hands without looking at the keyboard.

25 Always read two or more notes ahead, just like the way we read books, while we're reading a word we've already seen the next or the entire sentence.
It gives you a breezy read, Makes you read faster and gives you time to flip to the next page.

26 Play through the piece without stopping, Use you hearing to determine if you're off and don't stop or look down to your fingers.

27 If allowed duplicate the piece and make markings on the photocopy.

28 Practice sight singing and always keep your counting.

MODULATION

Modulation is a change of key in a musical piece.

We have different kinds of modulation, namely:

* GRADUAL MODULATION
* PARTIAL   MODULATION
* ABRUPT   MODULATION

Gradual Modulation is a change of Key to a nearest key above
or below, an example is from key C to C#.

Partial Modulation is a change of Key that is made and not quite
long returned to its original key, an example if from key C to C# and
back to key C.

Abrupt Modulation is a change of Key that is made to a distance
key that is above or below the original key, an example is from key C
to key F.

CIRCLES OF FIFTH

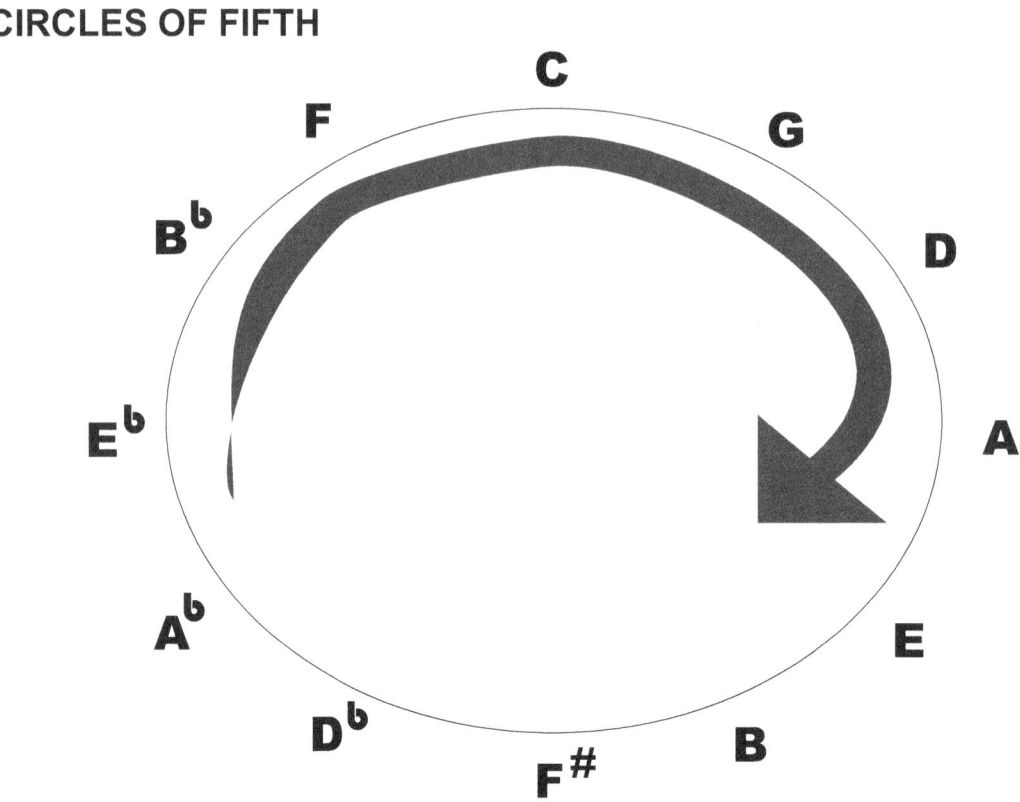

CIRCLES OF FOURTH

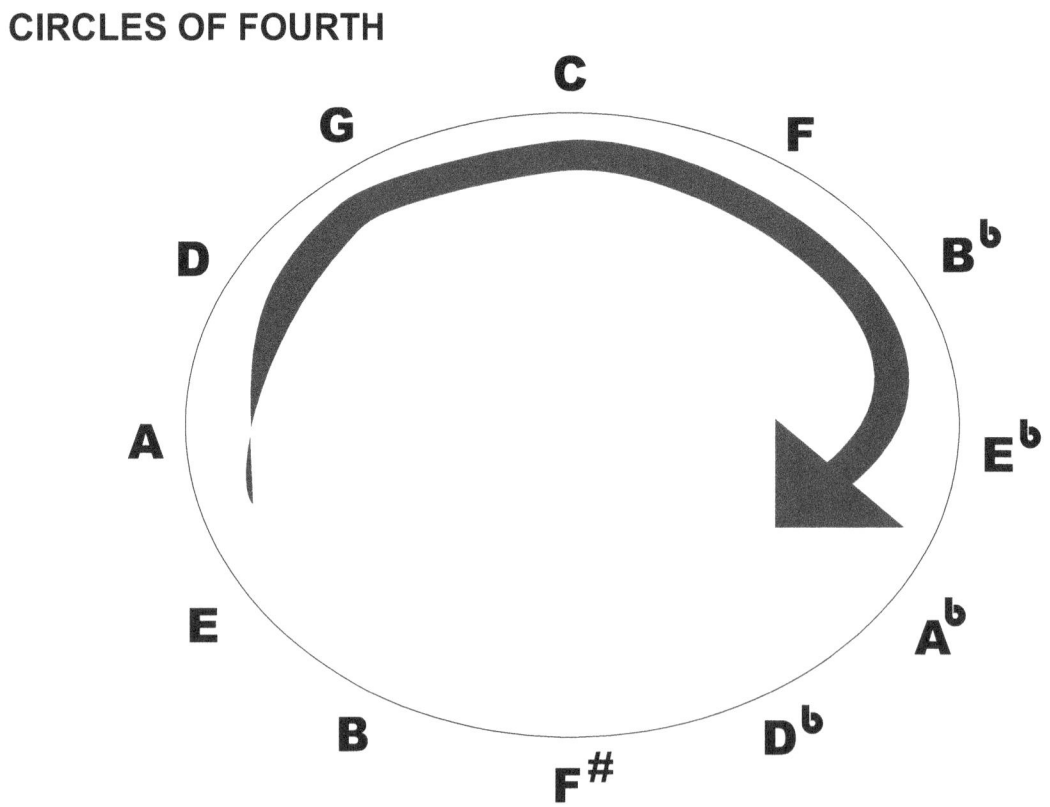

MUSICAL ALPHABET

Musical alphabet are the first seven letters in English alphabet:

A, B, C, D, E, F, G.

They are used to name the musical notes and identify piano keys.

MUSICAL NOTATION

Music notation are symbols used to write musical sound and its value, They are called notes.

PARTS OF THE NOTE

Up Note:

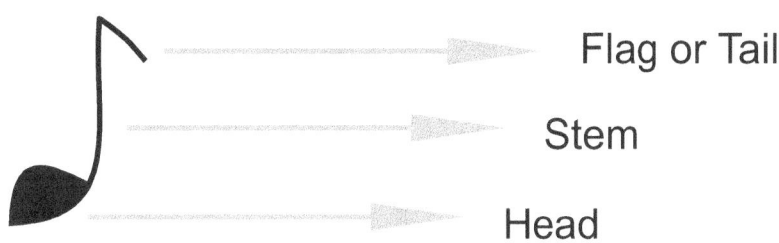

Flag or Tail

Stem

Head

Down Note:

Head

Stem

Flag or Tail

When you see a note placed over another it means Soprano and Auto are going to sing the same note.

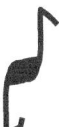

MUSICAL NOTATION VALUES BASED ON SHAPE

NAME	Shapes of Note	Value	Rest
Breve	\\|O\\|	8 bt	
Semi breve	O	4 bt	
Minim		2 bt	
Crotchet		1 bt	
Quaver		½ bt	
Semi Quaver		1/4 bt	
Demi Semi Quaver		1/8 bt	
Hemi Demi Semi Quaver		1/16 bt	

* Bt Means Beat, the number of count.

* Rest is moment of silent in a musical piece.

DOTTED NOTE

A dot placed after a note increases the note by half of its original value.

Example:

\|O\|.   **8 + 4 = 12 beat**

O.   **4 + 2 = 6 beat**

♪.   **2 + 1 = 3 beat**

DOUBLE DOTTED NOTE

\|O\|..   **8 + 4 + 2 = 14 beat**

O..   **4 + 2 + 1 = 7 beat**

♪..   **2 + 1 + 1/2 = 3 and 1/2 beat**

* The second dot increase the value of the first dot by half.

SIMPLE TIME SIGNATURE

Simple time signature are common counts, timing of a musical piece. There are three kinds of Simple Time Signature:

* SIMPLE DUPLE

* SIMPLE TRIPLE

* SIMPLE QUADRUPLE

SIMPLE DUPLE:
The upper figure is Two (2) while the lower figure could be 2, 4, 8, 16, 32...

$\frac{2}{2}$ (2 by 2) $\frac{2}{4}$ (2 by 4) $\frac{2}{8}$ (2 by 8) $\frac{2}{16}$ (2 by 16)

Examples of Notes:

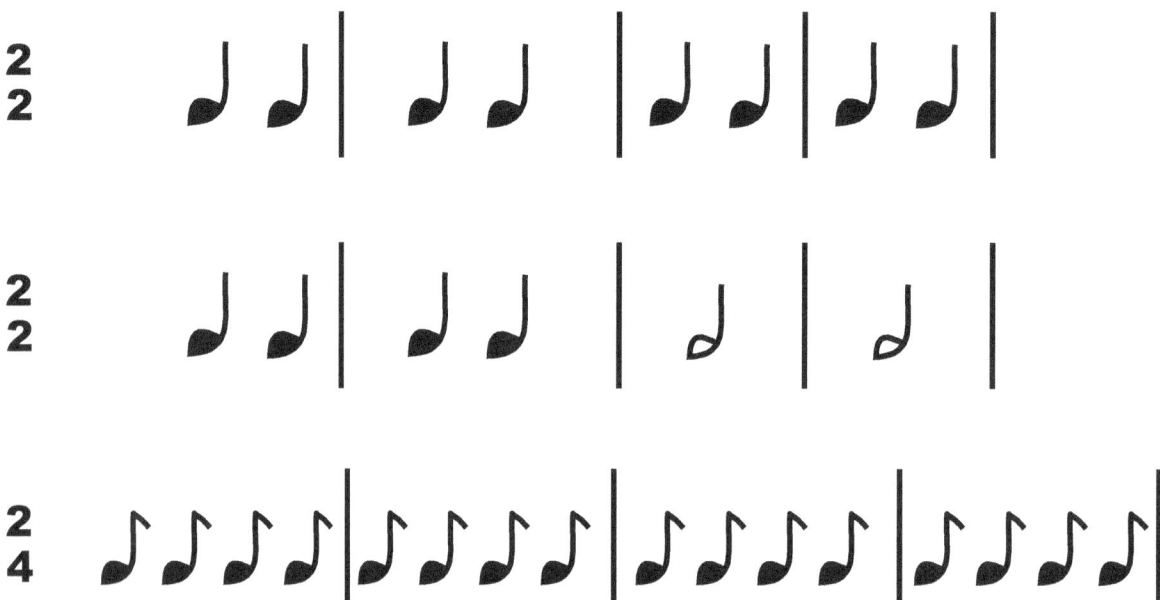

Count the beats with the use of a wall Clock movement sound; "TICK TAC".
*Preferably use a METRONOME for accurate timing.

SIMPLE TIME SIGNATURE

Examples of Notes:

$\frac{2}{8}$

$\frac{2}{16}$

SIMPLE TRIPLE:
The upper figure is Three (3) while lower figure could be 2, 4, 8, 16...

$\frac{3}{2}$ (3 by 2) $\frac{3}{4}$ (3 by 4) $\frac{3}{8}$ (3 by 8) $\frac{3}{16}$ (3 by 16)

Examples of Notes:

$\frac{3}{2}$

$\frac{3}{4}$

SIMPLE TIME SIGNATURE

SIMPLE QUADRUPLE: The upper figure is Four (4) while lower figure could be 2, 4, 8, 16...

$\frac{4}{2}$ (4 by 2) $\frac{4}{4}$ (4 by 4) $\frac{4}{8}$ (4 by 8) $\frac{4}{16}$ (4 by 16)

Examples of Notes:

* The Time Signature examples are for general knowledge purpose, as a Beginner or an Intermediate musician the common time signature you would come across more often is likely going to be the: **2 by 4,   3 by 4,   and   4 by 4** time signatures.

COMPOUND TIME SIGNATURE

Compound time signature are advance timing and counts of a musical piece, they are signatures that have their higher figures multiplied in:
* Twos for COMPOUND DUPLE

* Threes for COMPOUND TRIPLE

* Fours for COMPOUND QUADRUPLE

COMPOUND DUPLE:
The upper figure is Six (6) while the lower figure could be 2, 4, 8, 16, 32...

$\frac{6}{2}$ (6 by 2) $\frac{6}{4}$ (6 by 4) $\frac{6}{8}$ (6 by 8) $\frac{6}{16}$ (6 by 16)

Examples of Notes:

COMPOUND TRIPLE:
The upper figure is Nine (9) while the lower figure could be 2, 4, 8, 16, 32...

$\frac{9}{2}$ (9 by 2) $\frac{9}{4}$ (9 by 4) $\frac{9}{8}$ (9 by 8) $\frac{9}{16}$ (9 by 16)

COMPOUND TRIPLE:
The upper figure is Twelve (12) while the lower figure could be 2, 4, 8, 16, 32...

$\frac{12}{2}$ (12 by 2) $\frac{12}{4}$ (12 by 4) $\frac{12}{8}$ (12 by 8) $\frac{12}{16}$ (12 by 16)

Count the beats with the use of a wall Clock sound movement; "TICK TAC".

*Preferably use a METRONOME for accurate timing.

HOW TO BECOME A BETTER MUSICIAN

MUSIC THEORY - Is the study of how music works, it examines the Language, Notation and Style of music.

MUSIC PRODUCTION - Is the act of creating and making musical piece, through the art of sounds combination.

TYPES OF MUSIC (GENRES)

* classical music
* contemporary music
* jazz music
* reggae music
* r & b music
* soul music
* rock & roll music
* afro music
* pop music
* callipso music
* funky music
* salsa

* makosa music
* highlife music
* aria aria music
* oghene music
* juju music
* lullaby music
* bugi bugi music
* hip hop music
* acapela music
* folks music
* country music
* blues music

THINGS TO KNOW IN MUSIC WRITING

* TERMS: Not all pieces of music can be regarded as songs, because song has either text, lyrics or both.

An instrumental composition can be called a piece, work or a solo.

* CAPITALIZATION: Chronological period of music history is to be Capitalized (Classical era, Romantic piano, Baroque, the Renaissance)

Medieval period - are not to be capitalized.

* Genres of music are not to be capitalized use (rock, jazz, hip hop, blues funky. INSTEAD of:; Rock, Jazz, Hip Hop, Blues, Funky).

* Don't use wrong descriptive words in place of music terminology, words like "it's too rushing, instead think of why the music sounds rushing!, Is it the Tempo or Pitch?".

You could write or say play soft (piano/ pianissimo).

* Don't use mathematical counting numerals (1, 2, 3...) When numbering, instead use roman numerals i, ii, iii ..., For chord identification.

CHARACTERISTICS OF A MUSICAL SOUND

SOUND: is what comes out of the voice, as an effect of vibration. There are two type of sounds:

* MUSICAL SOUND
* NOISE   SOUND

A steady sound that can be interpreted is musical sound while the one without a regular frequency is a noise sound.

HUMAN VOICE: is sounds that comes from human as a result of Vocal vibration and gliding of the tongue.

ATTRIBUTE OF MUSICAL SOUND

* <u>TIMBER:</u>   Quality of sound produce

* <u>PITCH:</u>   Height and Depth of musical note.

* <u>INTENSITY:</u> Loudness and softness of a musical sound.

* <u>TEMPO:</u>   Speed of the music.

* <u>DURATION:</u> Timing and length of a music.

www.EzraCreativeProductions.com   In a World of Creation Where Ideas Come to Life...

52

VOICE TRAINING AND EXERCISES

Voice training is the art of enhancing and building the human voice to sound better, through good voice exercises and techniques.

It's also mastering the art of breathing and singing properly.

A VOICE TRAINER is also known as **A Voice Coach**, He or She is the one that takes you through the process of Voice training and its exercises until you master the art of singing, within an agreed period of time.

Dos & DON'T OF VOICE TRAINING
Are what to do and not to do in other to have and maintain a good Voice.

THINGS TO DO IN ORDER TO MAINTAIN AND IMPROVE THE VOICE

*   Drink enough water regularly

*   Take natural honey regularly

*   Eat fruits/ Beverages

*   If you can, Drink tiled milk or raw egg

*   Eat fresh Pepper

*   Regular stretching and body exercise

*   Yoga and meditation

*   Resting of the Voice

*   Try mimicking professionals, those you love their, sound, style of music and way of singing, it sharpens your ability to sing, bring out the best in you.

Dos & DON'T OF VOICE TRAINING

The opposite of what to do in other to improve and enhance the Voice is what not to do in other to maintain and keep a good voice.

SOME OF THE THINGS TO AVOID IN ORDER TO MAINTAIN A GOOD VOICE

* Avoid shouting (Noise and noise makers!)

* Cold Water, Drinks

* Ice

* Too much starchy foods

* Oily & Fried foods

* Roasted Corns

* Too much Coconut

* Bones

* Biscuits

* Any food that its particles would stick to your throat, or could pierce your throat while or after eating eating it is not good for the voice and should be avoided, or be taken in a very minimal quantity when necessary.

What to do in other to improve and enhance the Voice is what not to do in other to maintain and keep a good voice.

BREATHING EXERCISES

Breathing is the process in which we take in air through our Nostrils or Mouth known as Oxygen and release of this air back to our environment as carbon dioxide.

In other words breathing is the process of taking in and release of air. As much as breathing is needed for survival (Living) it's also a vital aspect of singing technique that one needs to master in other to bring out the beauty in their voice and its uniqueness.

It is said that if you can breath well then you can sing well

If your breathing is right, then your singing will be right. It is your breathing that makes availability of air which vibrates and turns into waves, It's your breathing that produces and sustains your sound.

Proper breathing helps to exhale fear, nervousness and helps you stand tall.

STEPS FOR BREATHING EXERCISE

* STANDING:
    Stand straight breathing and store the air in your stomach,
    hold the breath fo ten seconds and exhale.

  repeat the exercise many times, afterwards increase the time you hold the air without raising your shoulders to fifteen, twenty thirty seconds.

* Repeat exercise while standing and seating, in different positions with your Legs closed together and apart.

* SIPPING IN OF AIR:
    Sip in air through the mouth ten times and sip out
    ten times, repeat the exercise and change the times of sipping of this air.

BREATHING EXERCISES

*   CORNER BREATHING:
    Bend left and right, side ways, front and back,
    When you bend stay in that position for some moments while you
    breath in air and hold your breath for ten seconds and breath out,
    repeat it three to five times, then change to another bent position,
    breath in and hold your breath then release the air after ten seconds.

Repeat the whole exercise again and increase the number of seconds you
hold your breath from Ten to Fifteen and Twenty

*   LIE DOWN:
    Lie down with your Tummy and repeat the exercise of
    breathing in and out while holding your breath for number of seconds
    like Ten seconds afterward increase the number of seconds.

    Lie down flat on you back facing up, breath in and hold your breath for
    Ten seconds, and release the air, repeat exercise five times while
    changing the duration you hold your breath from Ten to Fifteen.

*   PLACE A LIGHTWEIGHT ON TUMMY:
    Place some lightweight objects or books on your tummy while you
    breath in of air through your Nostrils and hold your breath for Ten
    seconds then release the air.

Repeat the exercise Five times and Close your Nostrils with your hand,
and Repeat the whole exercise again, while breathing through your Mouth.

*   BLOWING OF AIR:
    Blow out air until you fill empty and hold your
    breath for Fifteen Seconds, then release air and repeat the exercise.

BREATHING EXERCISES

57

*   Do general body exercise to look good and be fit, It strengthens your
     Vocal chords and helps you to project and sing better with Confidence.

*   RUNNING:
     Run Forth and Backward in a short distance,
     Try holding your breath as you run and only release it when you get to
     the other end.

Repeat the Exercise above while WALKING, Take a deep breath and hold
your breath as you walk for about Fifteen foot-steps and release the air,
Take another deep breath and always remember to store the air in your
STOMACH and not your chest or shoulders!.

<u>NOTE</u>
:
***   Repeat all the exercise above and make it a daily ROUTINE,

***   If any of the exercise mentioned above is not good for you stick to the
        ones that work best for you.

***   You are not obligated to complete or do any of the exercises if it's not good
       for you; it's a matter of preference, not compulsion.

www.EzraCreativeProductions.com   In a World of Creation Where Ideas Come to Life...

57

VOICE TRAINING EXERCISE WITH SOL - FA NOTES

One of the best ways to train your Voice and get instant feedback is by recording yourself as you sing in other to listen and analyze afterwards also with the aid of Computer software to help you see live analysis as you sing and train your Voice, and determine if you're getting it right or not, flatting or shifting out of line.

But in the absence of Voice analyzers and computer programs, you can train preferably with the PIANO, it's one of the most popular instrument used for Voice training exercise.

If you can't play the piano yourself, higher the service of a professional, Pianist or Voice Coach.

In the absence of a Professional ask a friend (someone you know that can play the piano) to help play some of the sol - fa notes below and you Hum or pronounce each sound heard.

I always tell people that "If you can sound like the piano you'll sing well and rightly harmonize pitches".

* PRACTICE with the Tonic Sol-fa in an ascending order.

  * Exercise One: **do, re, mi, fa, so, la, ti, do.**

Practice it in descending order:

  * Exercise Two: **do, ti, la, so, fa, mi, re, do.**

* Three: **do, ti, la, so, fa, mi, re, do, ti, la, so, fa, mi, re, do.**

* PRACTICE with the first five sol - fa notes in ascending order long enough

  * Exercise Four: **do, re, mi, fa, so.**

Practice in descending order pronounce the sound with your Voice "Loud"

  * Exercise Five: **so, fa, mi, re, do.**

TRAINING EXERCISE WITH SOL - FA NOTES

PRACTICE with the Major chord Sol - fa note:

* Exercise Six: **do, re, mi, fa, so, fa, mi, re, do.**

* Exercise Seven: **do, mi, so**

* Exercise Eight: **so, mi, do**

* Exercise Nine: **do, mi, so, mi**

* Ex Ten: d, r, d, m, d, f, d, s, d, l, d, t, d, d, d, t, d, l, d, s, d, f, d, m, d, r, d.

* Look up for new exercises on the Keyboard online and Music library.

RIGHT HAND
(Exercise One)

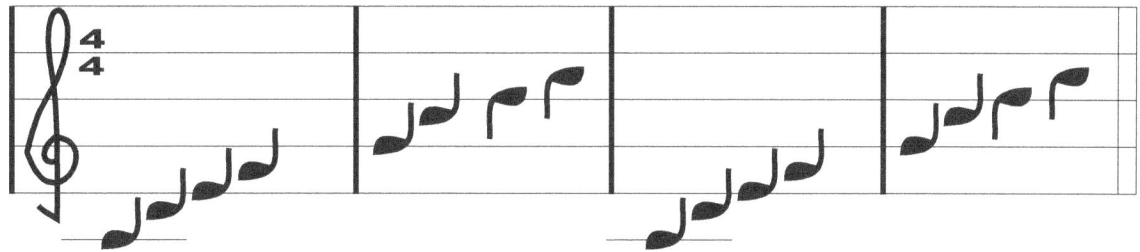

(Exercise Two)

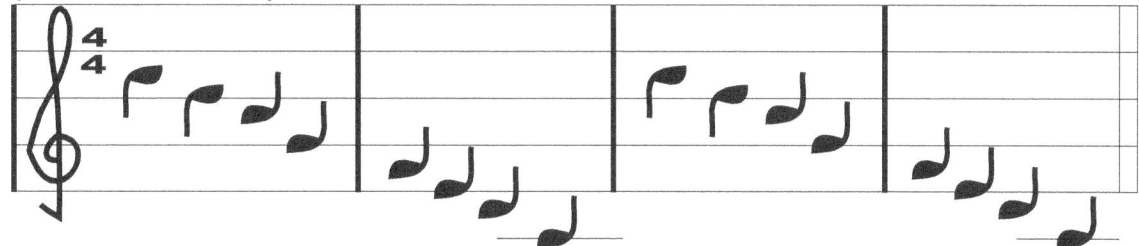

(Exercise Three)

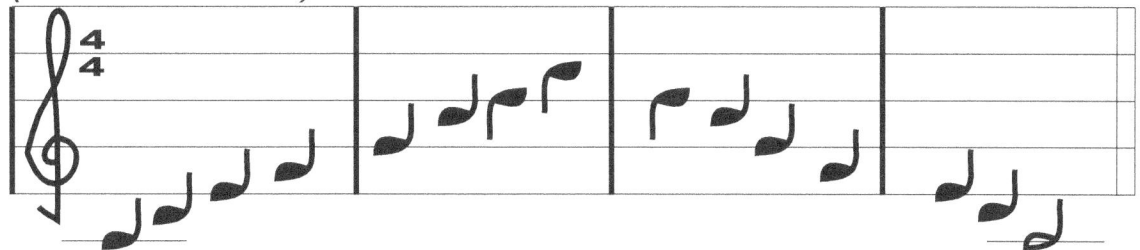

TRAINING EXERCISE WITH SOL - FA NOTES

RIGHT HAND

(Exercise Four)

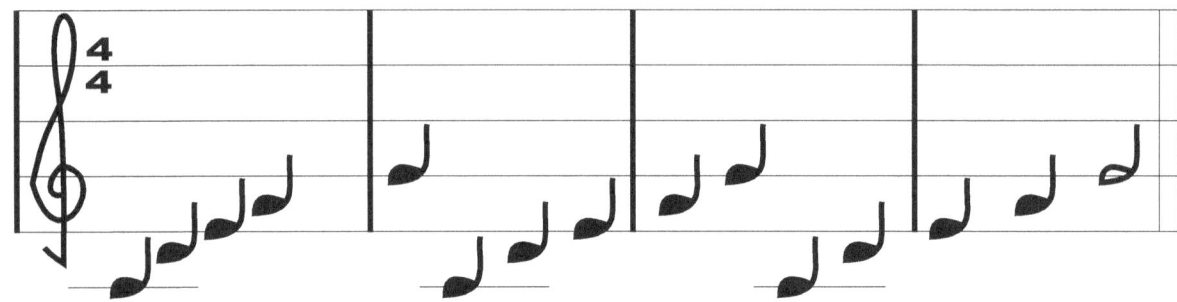

(Exercise Five)

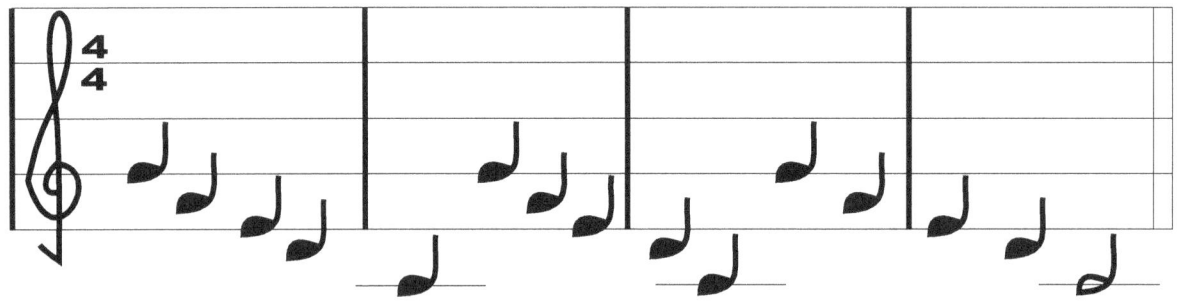

(Exercise Six)

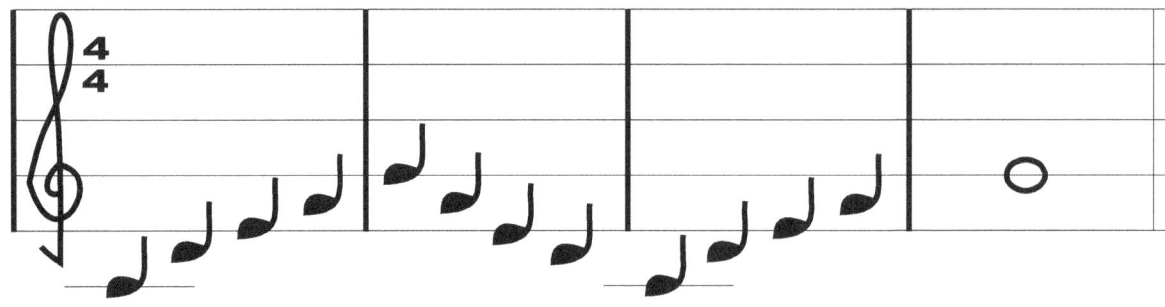

(Exercise Seven)

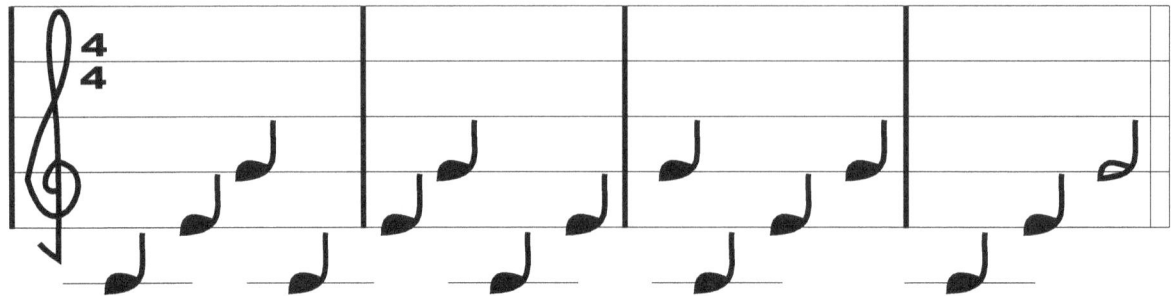

TRAINING EXERCISE WITH SOL - FA NOTES

RIGHT HAND

(Exercise Eight)

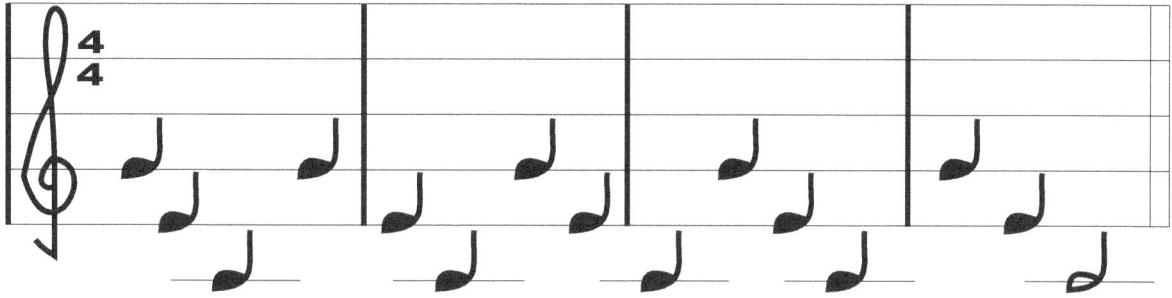

(Exercise Nine)

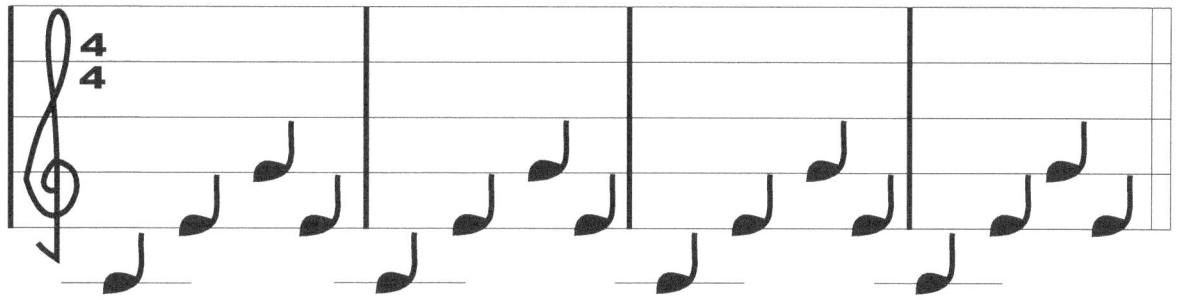

(Exercise Ten)

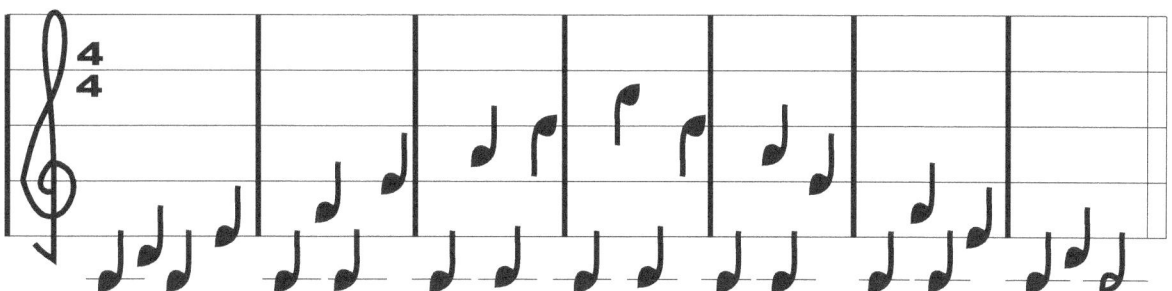

*   Practice each exercise for about Five minutes daily before going to the next exercise.

Start slow and gradually increase your speed of playing them after practicing long enough.

TRAINING EXERCISE WITH SOL - FA NOTES

<u>LEFT HAND</u>

(Exercise One)

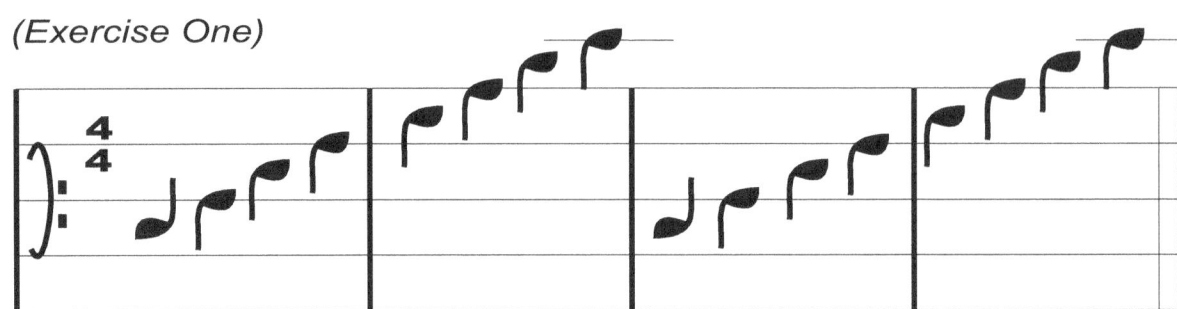

(Exercise Two)

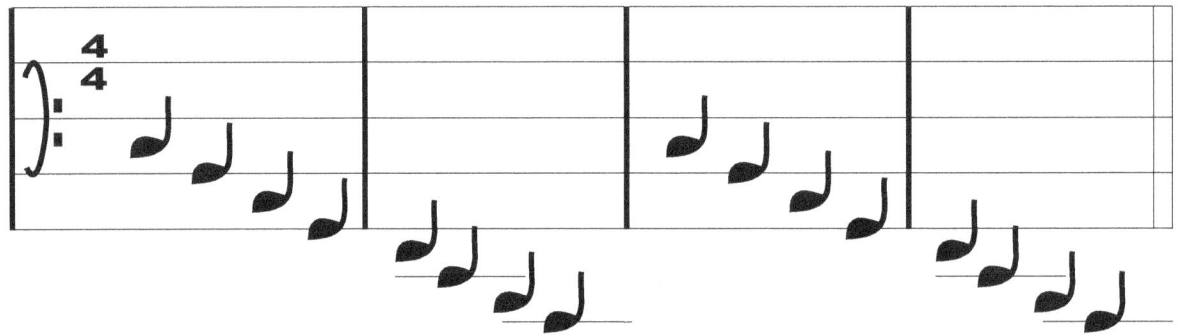

(Exercise Three)

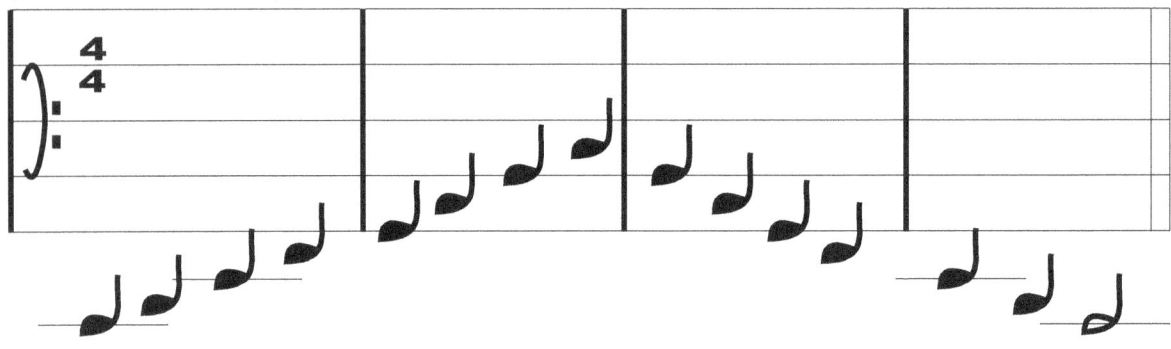

(Exercise Four)

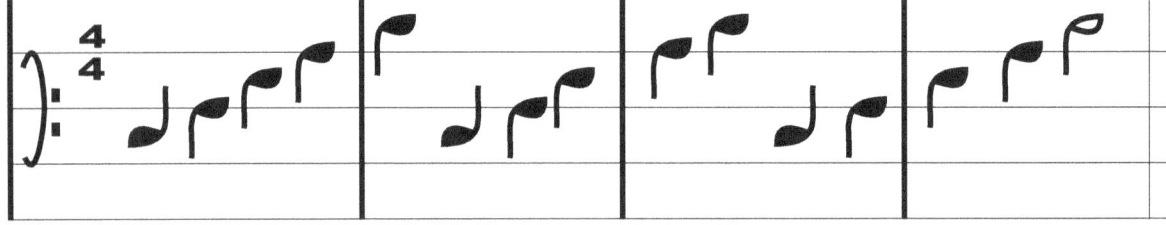

TRAINING EXERCISE WITH SOL - FA NOTES

<u>LEFT HAND</u>

(Exercise Five)

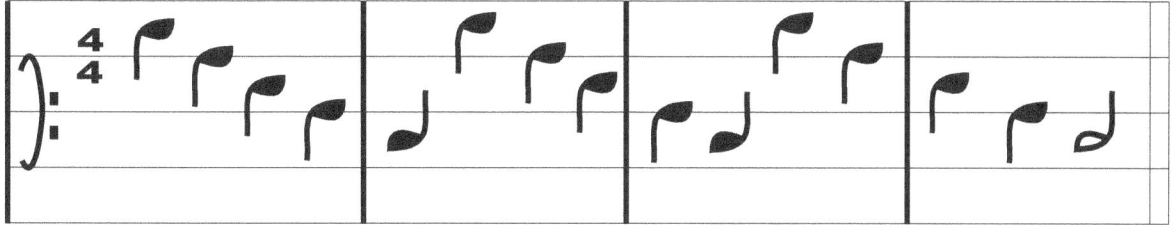

(Exercise Six)

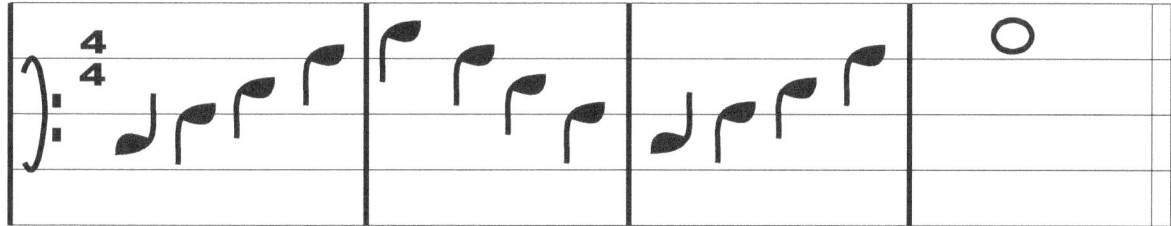

(Exercise Seven)

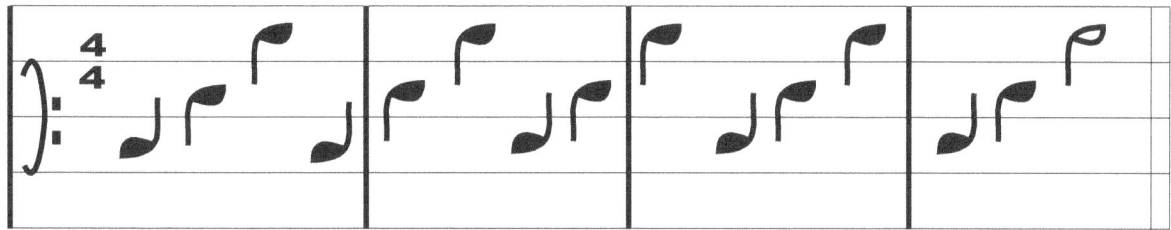

(Exercise Eight)

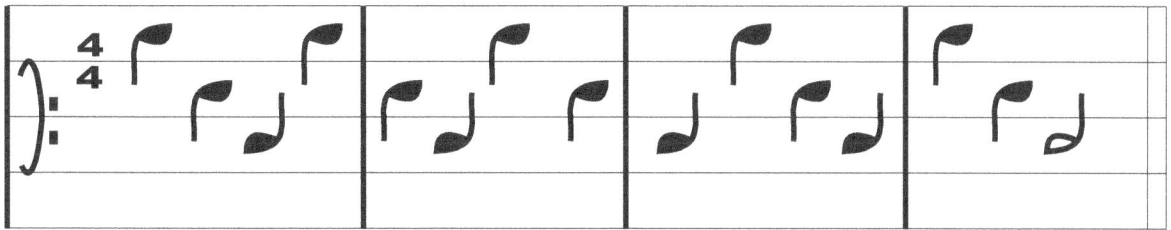

TRAINING EXERCISE WITH SOL - FA NOTES

LEFT HAND

(Exercise Nine)

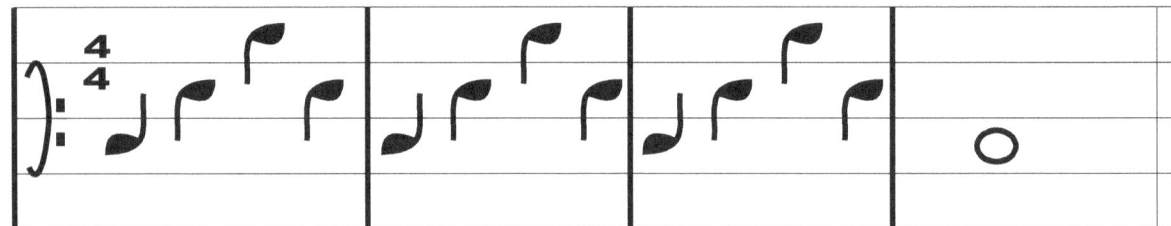

(Exercise Ten)

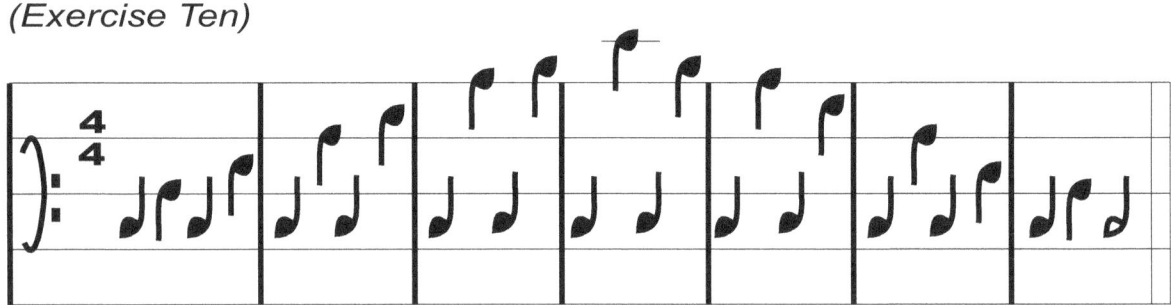

*   If you've practiced all the exercise long enough, good now is the time to play them on both hands simultaneously.

TRAINING EXERCISE ON BOTH HANDS

(Exercise One)

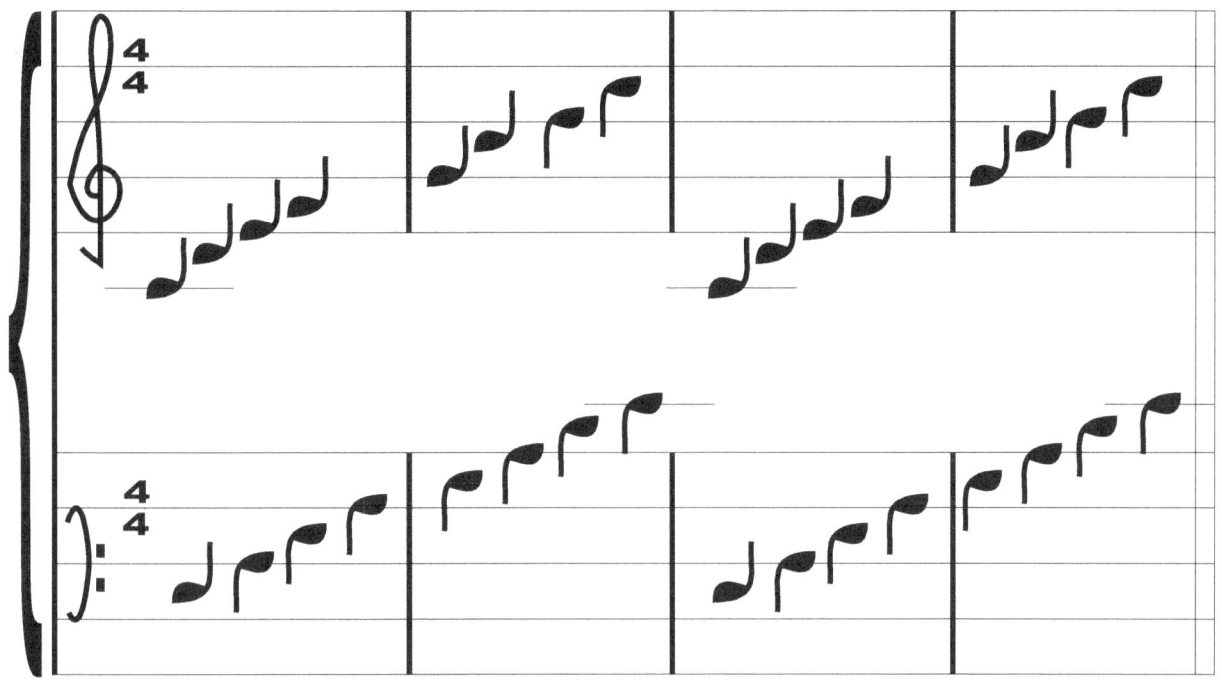

(Exercise Two)

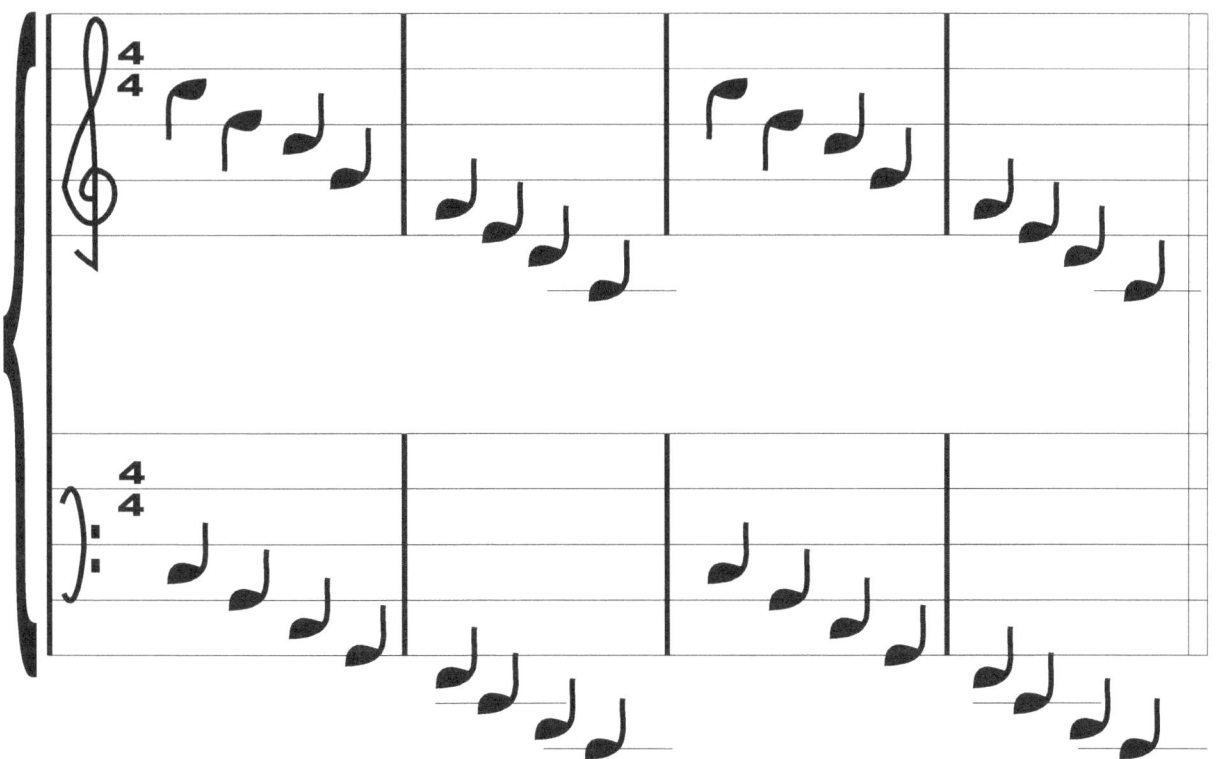

TRAINING EXERCISE ON BOTH HANDS

(Exercise Three)

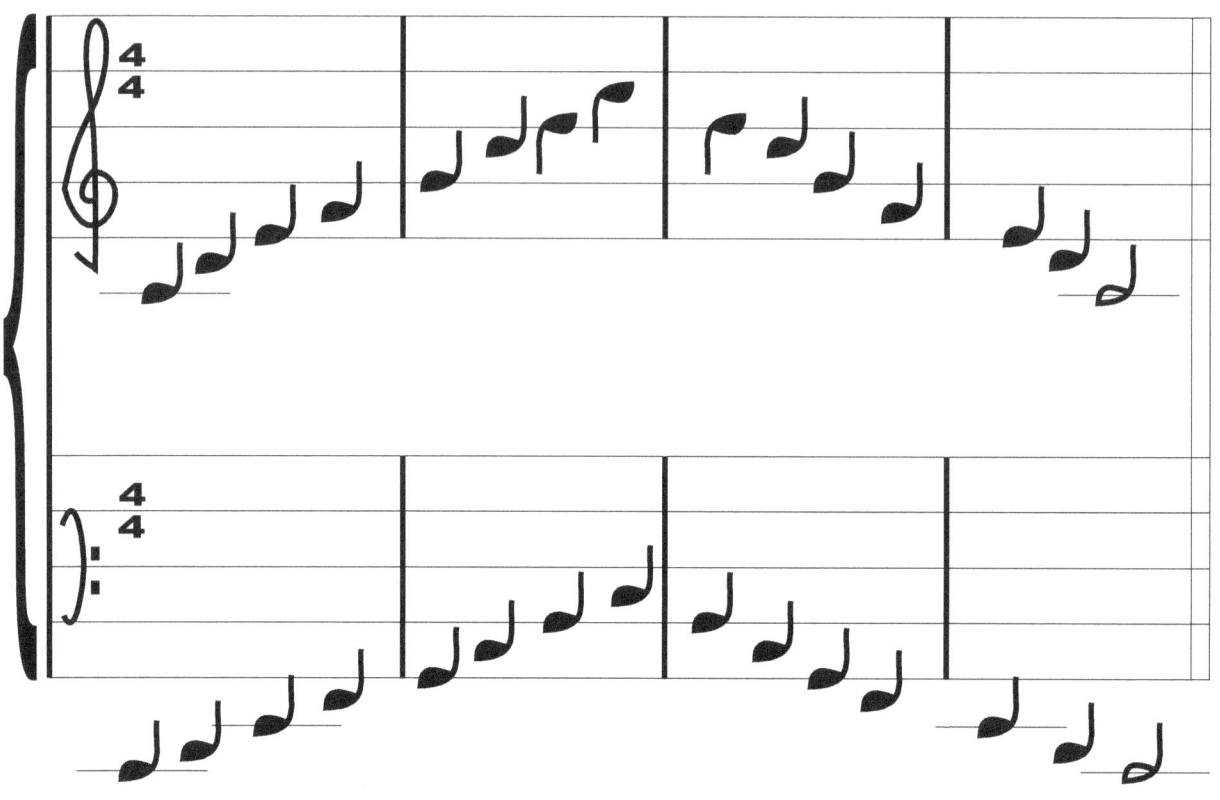

(Exercise Four)

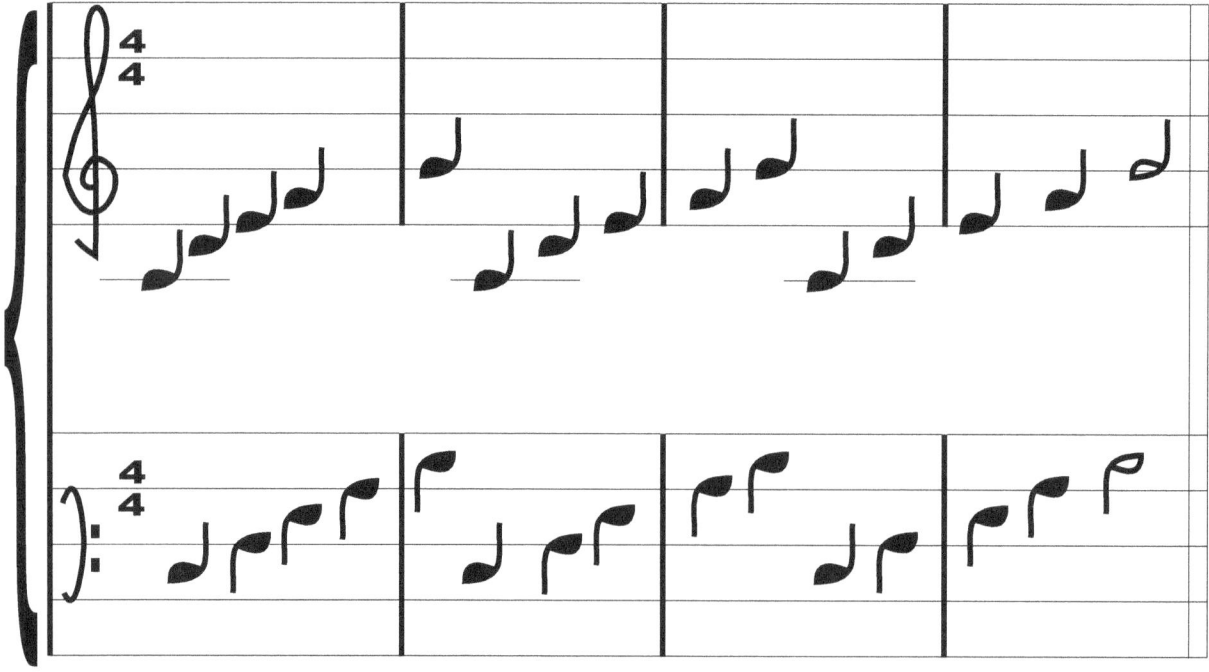

TRAINING EXERCISE ON BOTH HANDS

(Exercise Five)

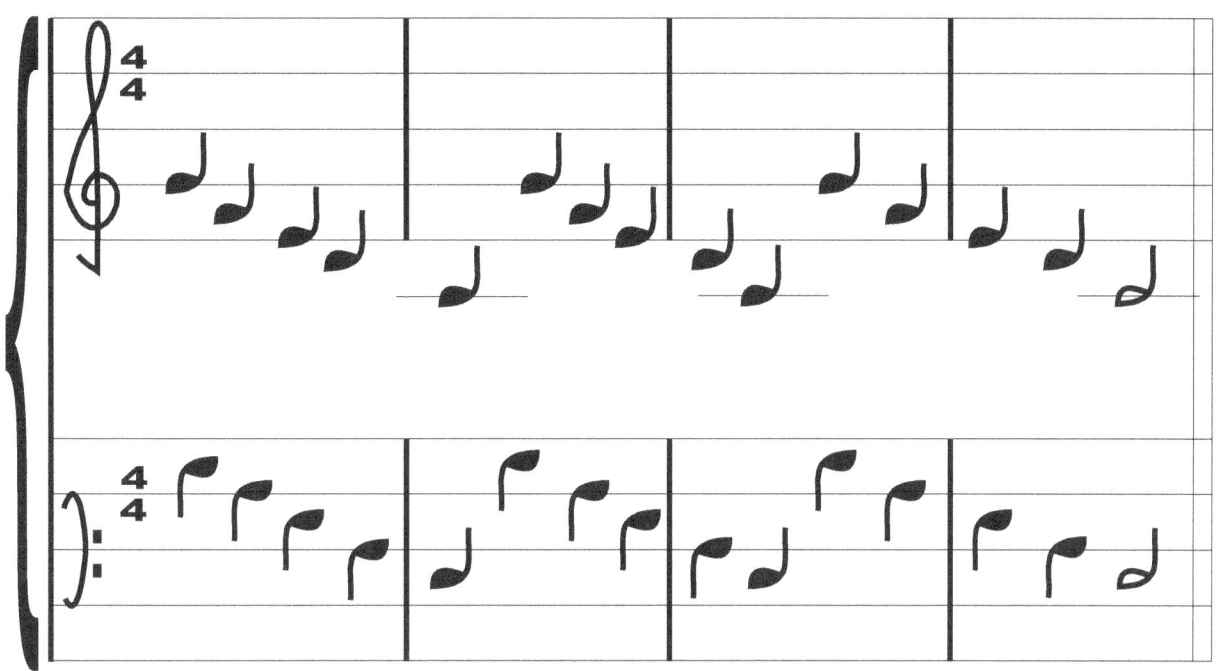

(Exercise Six)

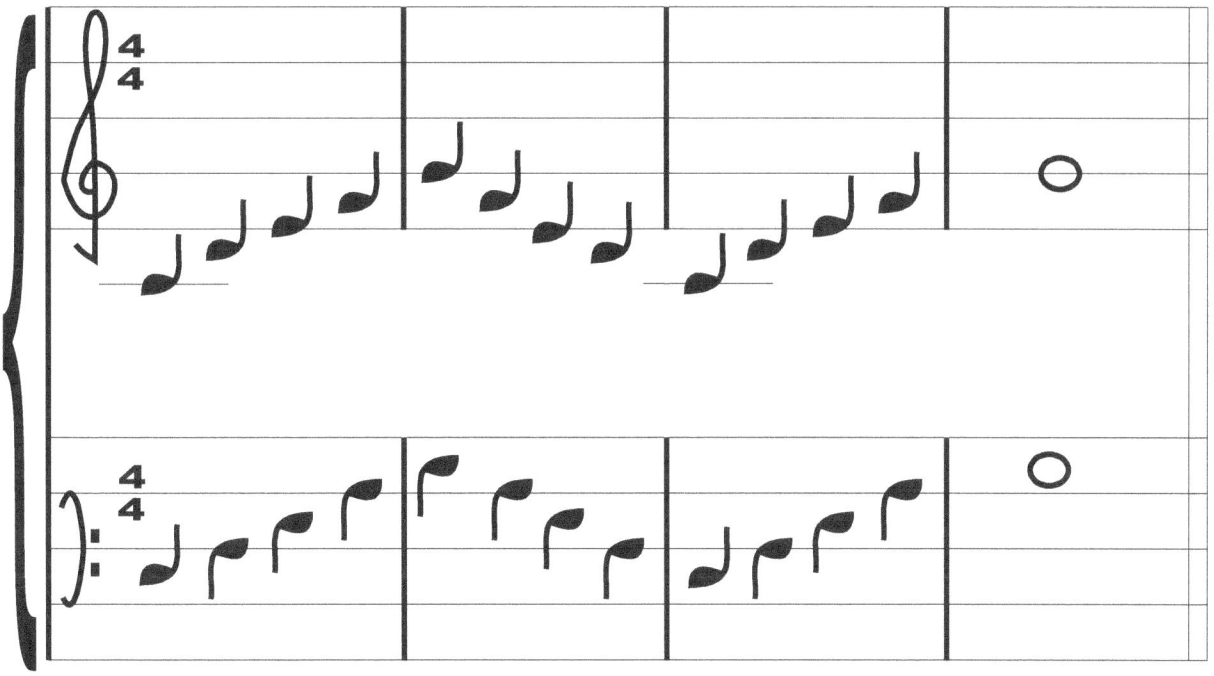

TRAINING EXERCISE ON BOTH HANDS

(Exercise Seven)

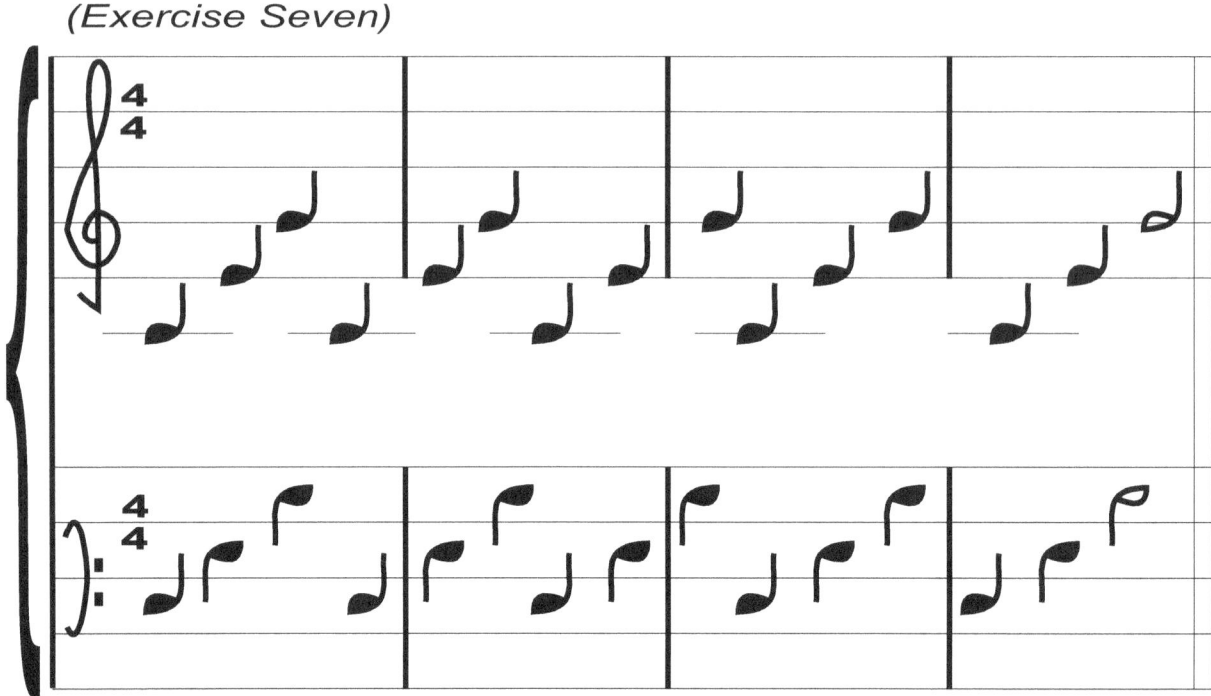

(Exercise Eight)

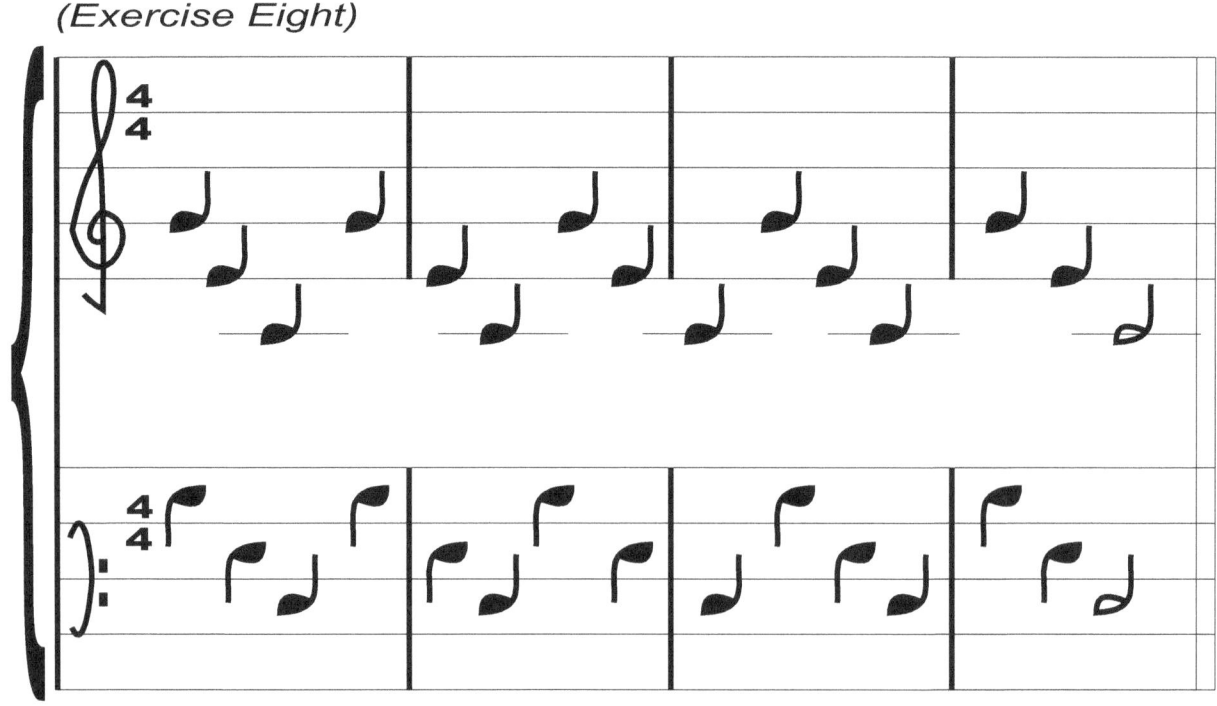

TRAINING EXERCISE ON BOTH HANDS

(Exercise Nine)

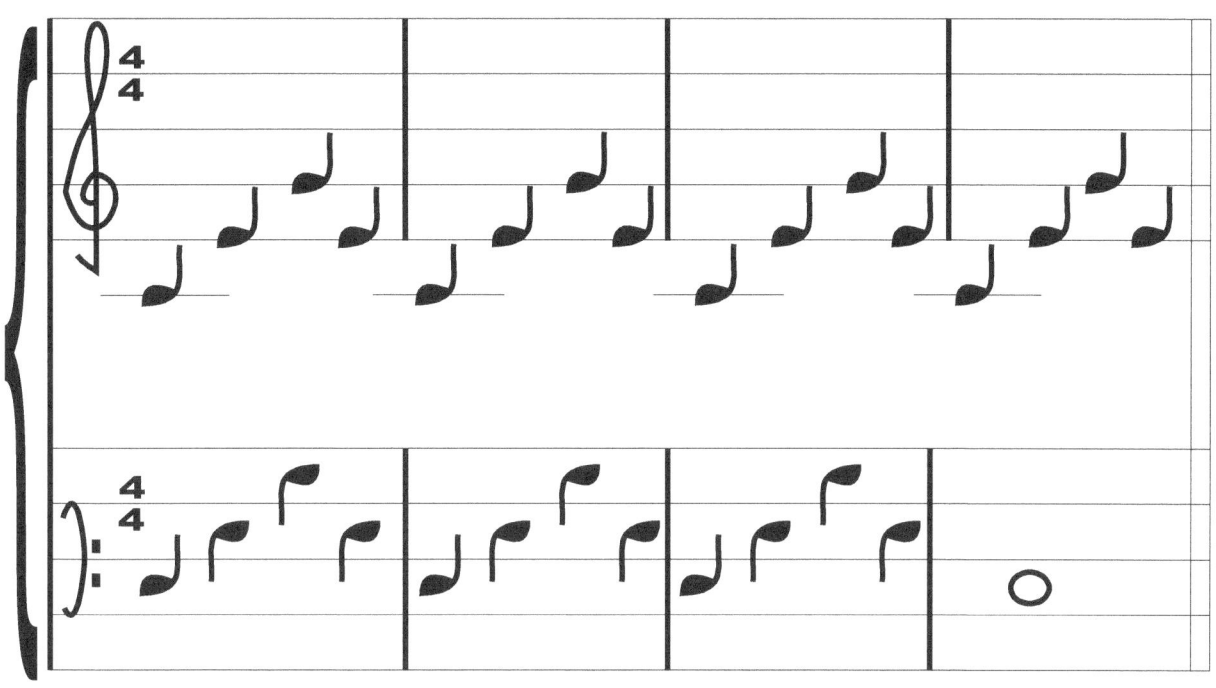

(Exercise Ten)

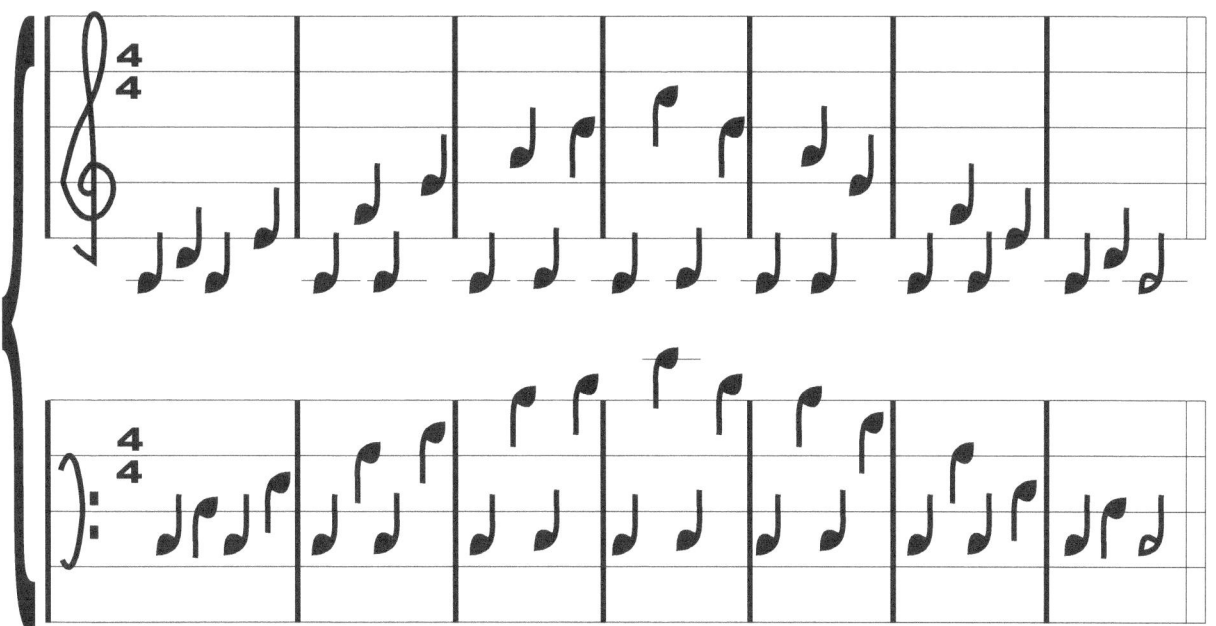

STAGE MANAGEMENT

Good use of your space when performing, make maximum use of the space allocated to you and be time conscious, don't exceed the time given to you, know when to start and when to end your performance.

* Select songs that matches your Vocal range and voice texture, don't choose songs that would be best sang by a tenor singer if you are a Soprano singer.

* Breath well before going up stage, remember good breathing leads to success in performance and accurate timing.

* Be in your confidence position, an excellent posture that doesn't project fear, because God has not given us the spirit of fear but of boldness, and sound mind.

* Rest while singing, it's a skill that needs to be learnt and mastered, while singing rest your voice in between your performance

* Use hand signals to convey messages to your crew on and off stage, for a change of Key, music tempo and Volume in a nice and stylish way, also for when to stop and for other vital instructions.

* Use of Diction is a key to great performance, learn to always pronounce your wordings out and clearly for the audience to hear, DON'T sing with your noise.

EXPRESSION

* If the song you're singing, or playing don't minister to you first it wouldn't get through any body, BE EXPRESSIVE as you sing.

* Hear yourself cause if you don't nobody will hear you.

* Think of the wordings you're singing, the song you're playing, what does it say to you, what's the message in it?
Know what it means and be conscious of what you minister say to people while on stage.

* Know your KEY, as a Singer, Pianist or an Organist you should be able to attempt and sing or play on all Keys but knowing your comfortable Key helps you build confidence and gives you room to express yourself.

RIGHT FINGERING OF MAJOR SCALE ON STAVE

* The numbers on each musical note indicates the proper finger to use.

Play with the Right hand first, then Left hand, after mastering the proper fingering of the Major Scale on separate hands try and play the scale with both hands at the same time .

RIGHT HAND FINGERING OF MAJOR SCALE ON <u>KEY</u> **C**

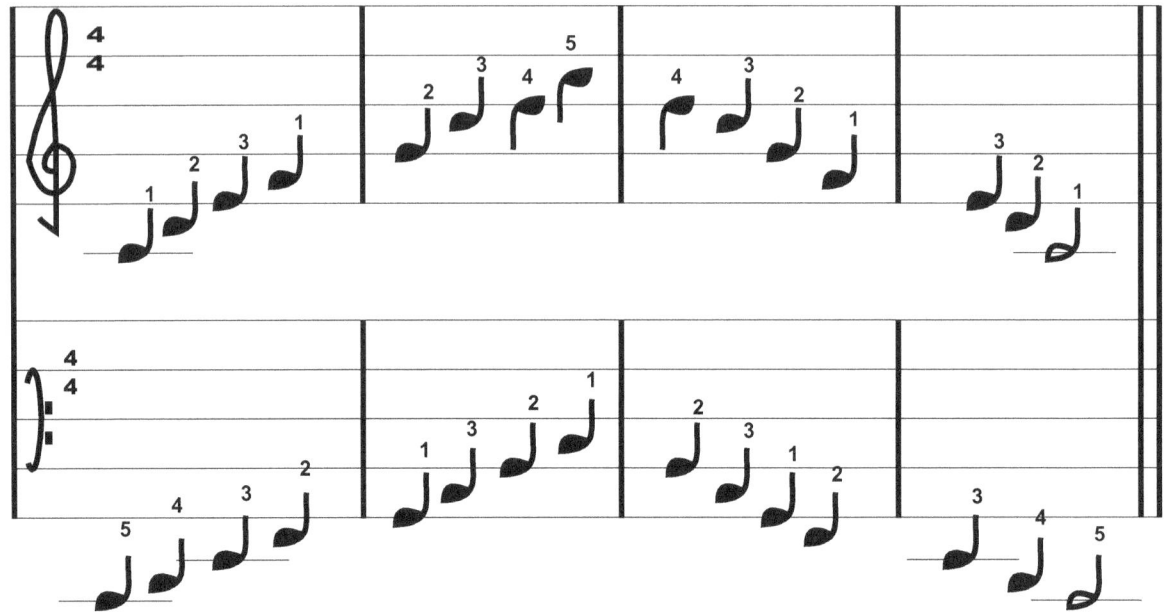

RIGHT HAND FINGERING OF MAJOR SCALE ON <u>Key</u> **Db**

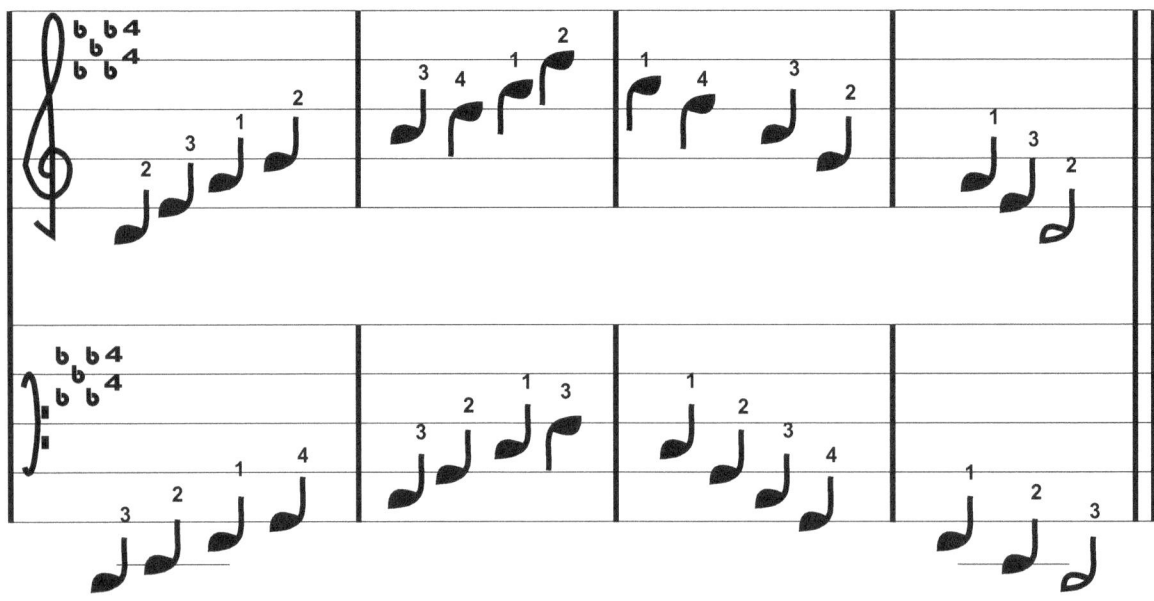

RIGHT FINGERING OF MAJOR SCALE ON STAVE

RIGHT HAND FINGERING OF MAJOR SCALE ON <u>KEY</u> **D**

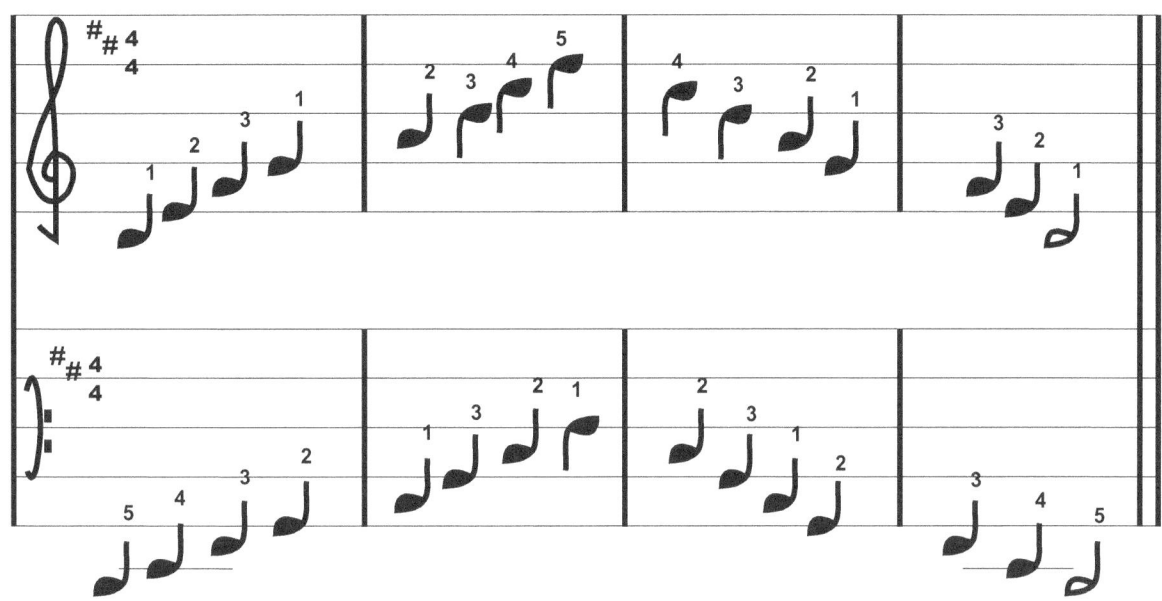

RIGHT HAND FINGERING OF MAJOR SCALE ON <u>KEY</u> **Eb**

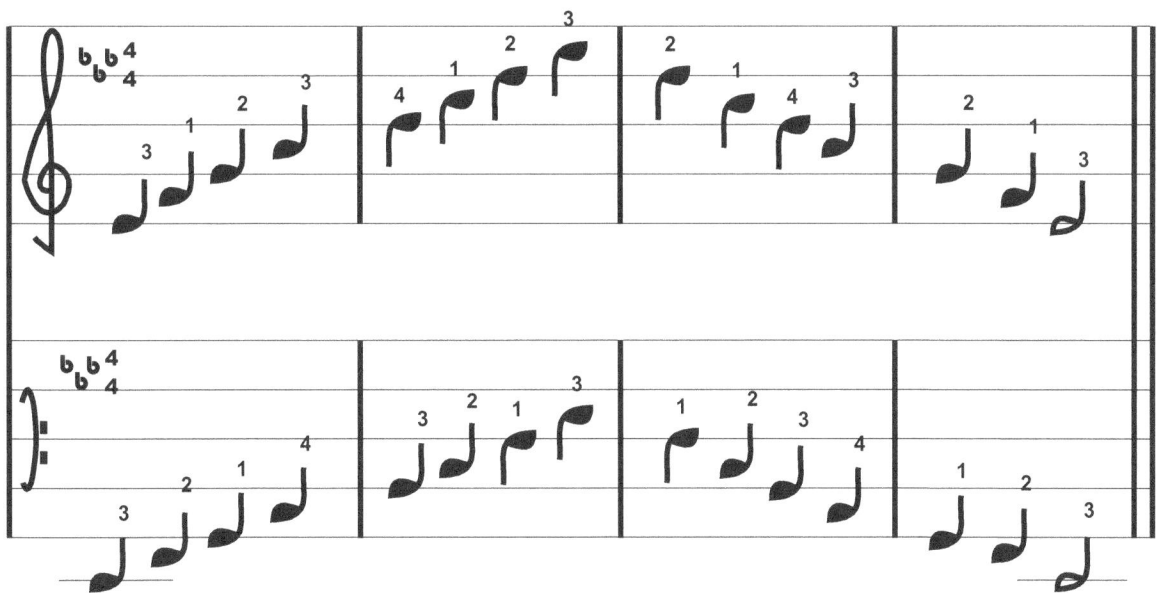

*   The numbers on each musical note indicates the proper finger to use.

Play with the Right hand first, then Left hand, after mastering the proper fingering of the Major Scale on separate hands try and play the scale with both hands. .

RIGHT FINGERING OF MAJOR SCALE ON STAVE

RIGHT HAND FINGERING OF MAJOR SCALE ON <u>KEY</u> **E**

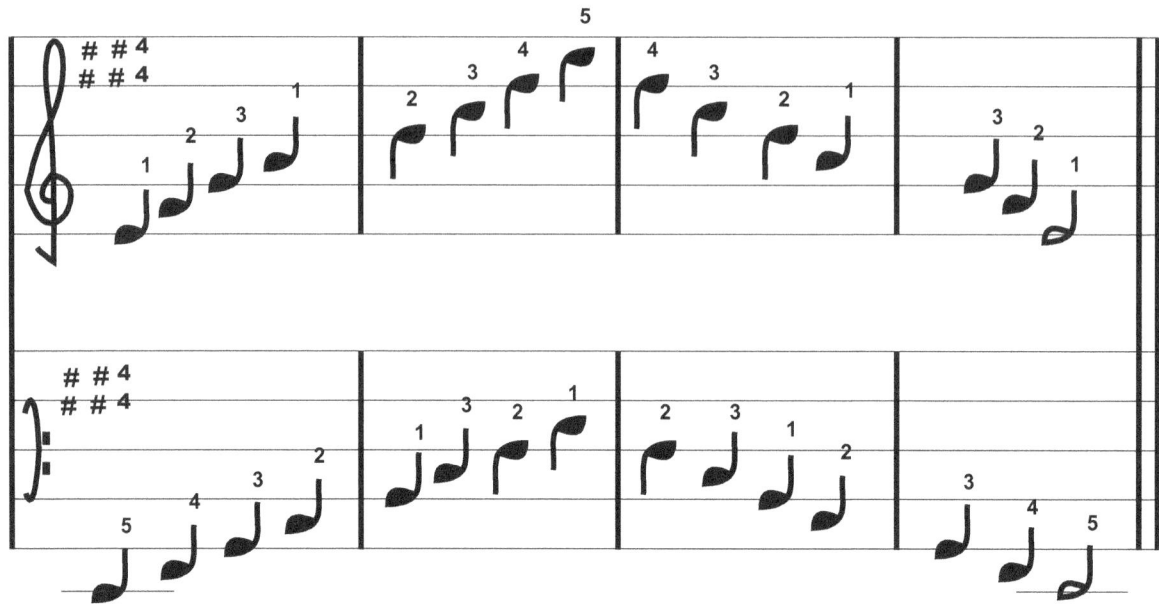

RIGHT HAND FINGERING OF MAJOR SCALE ON <u>KEY</u> **F**

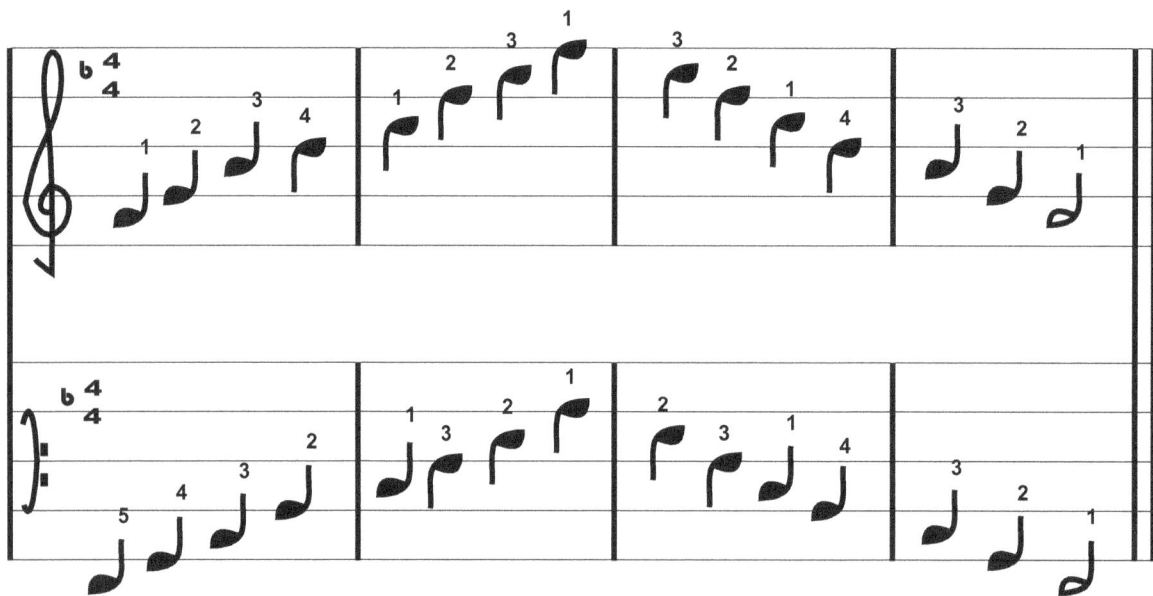

*   The numbers on each musical note indicates the proper finger to use.

Play with the Right hand first, then Left hand, after mastering the proper fingering of the Major Scale on separate hands try and play the scale with both hands. .

RIGHT FINGERING OF MAJOR SCALE ON STAVE

RIGHT HAND FINGERING OF MAJOR SCALE ON KEY **F#**

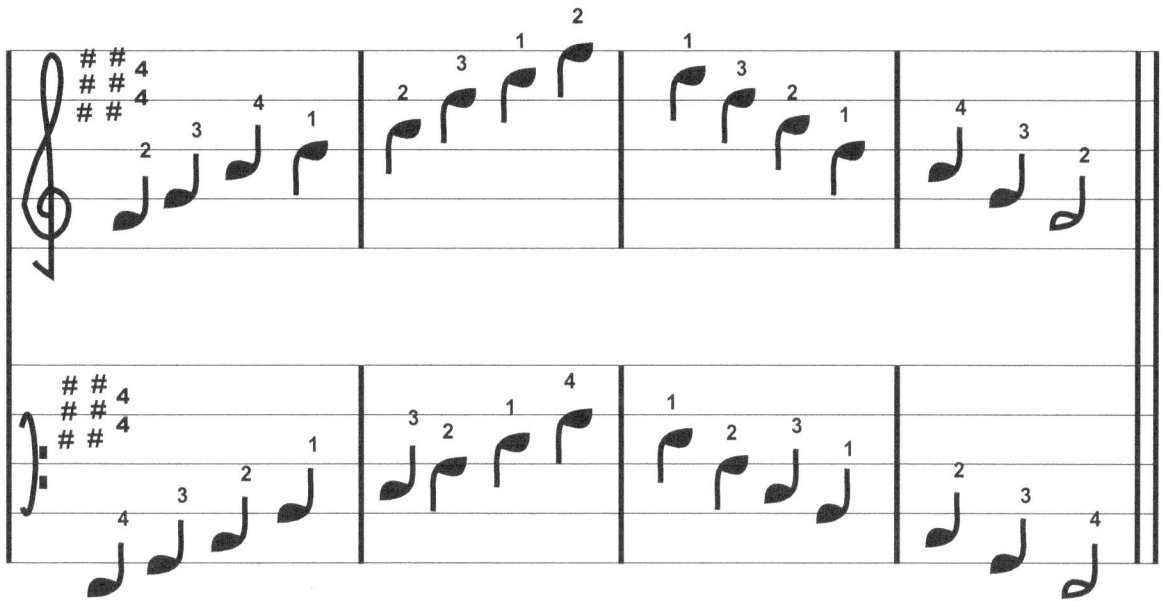

RIGHT HAND FINGERING OF MAJOR SCALE ON KEY **G**

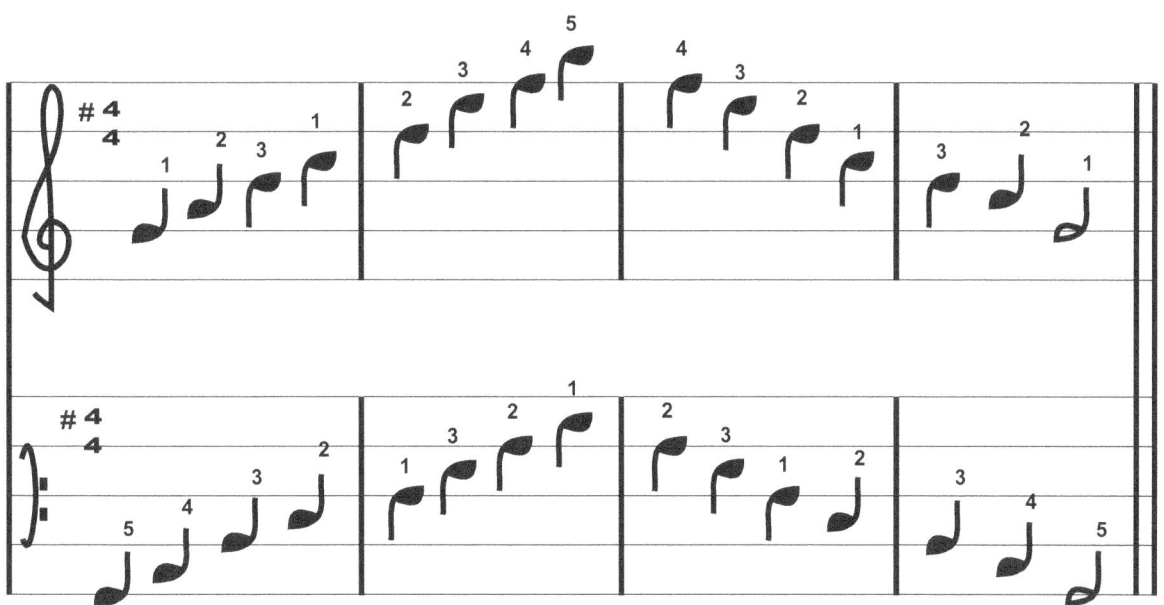

*   The numbers on each musical note indicates the proper finger to use.

Play with the Right hand first, then Left hand, after mastering the proper fingering of the Major Scale on separate hands try and play the scale with both hands. .

RIGHT FINGERING OF MAJOR SCALE ON STAVE

RIGHT HAND FINGERING OF MAJOR SCALE ON KEY **Ab**

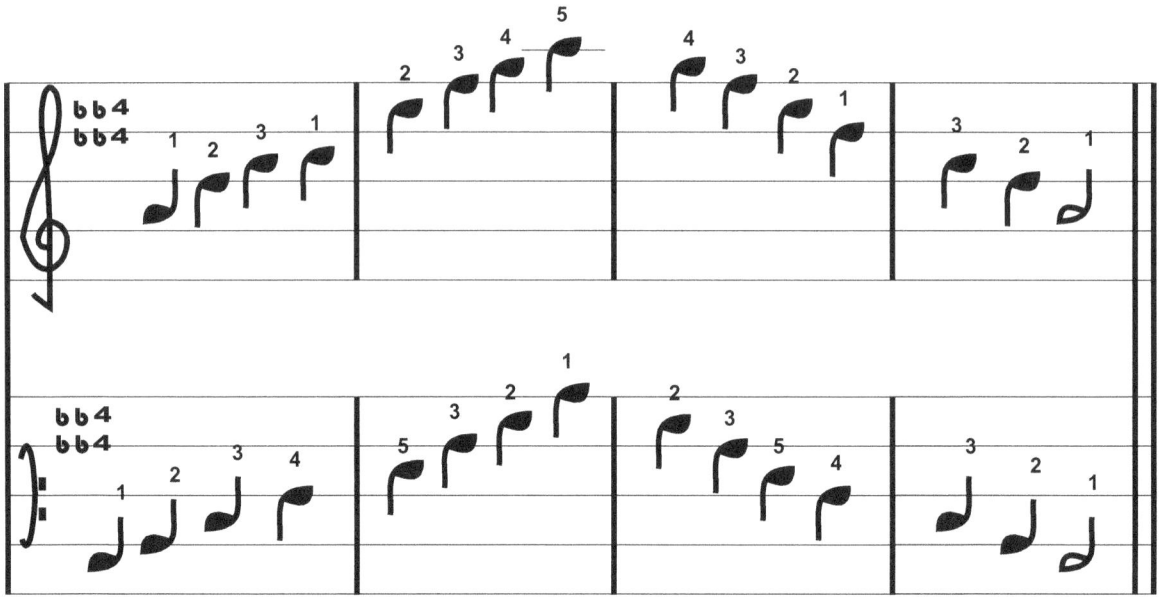

RIGHT HAND FINGERING OF MAJOR SCALE ON KEY **A**

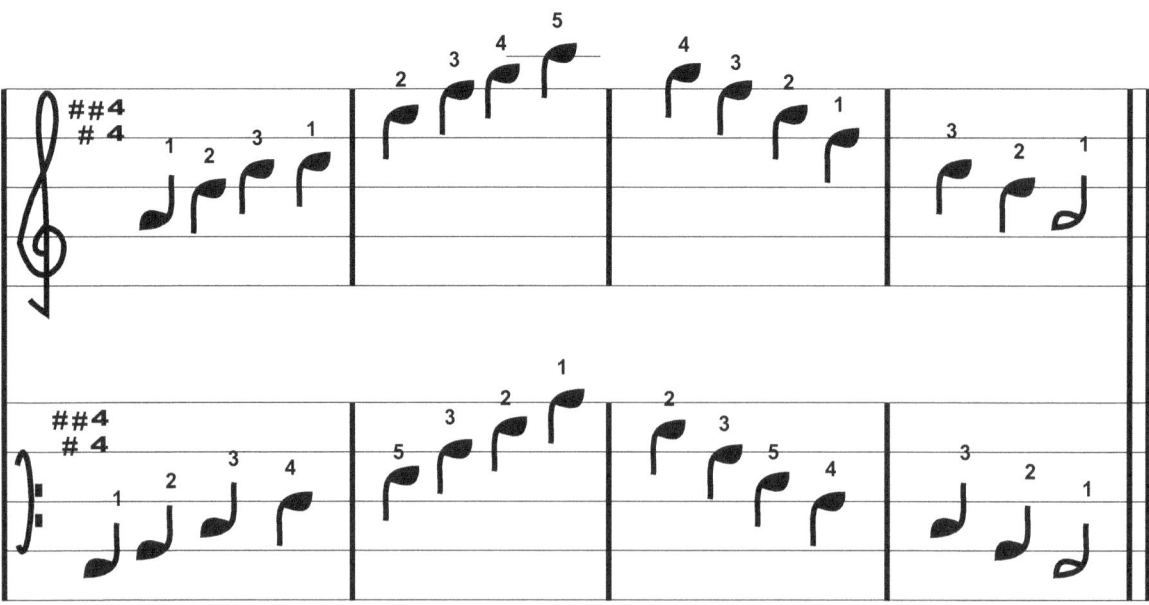

*   The numbers on each musical note indicates the proper finger to use.

Play with the Right hand first, then Left hand, after mastering the proper fingering of the Major Scale on separate hands try and play the scale with both hands. .

RIGHT FINGERING OF MAJOR SCALE ON STAVE

RIGHT HAND FINGERING OF MAJOR SCALE ON KEY **Bb**

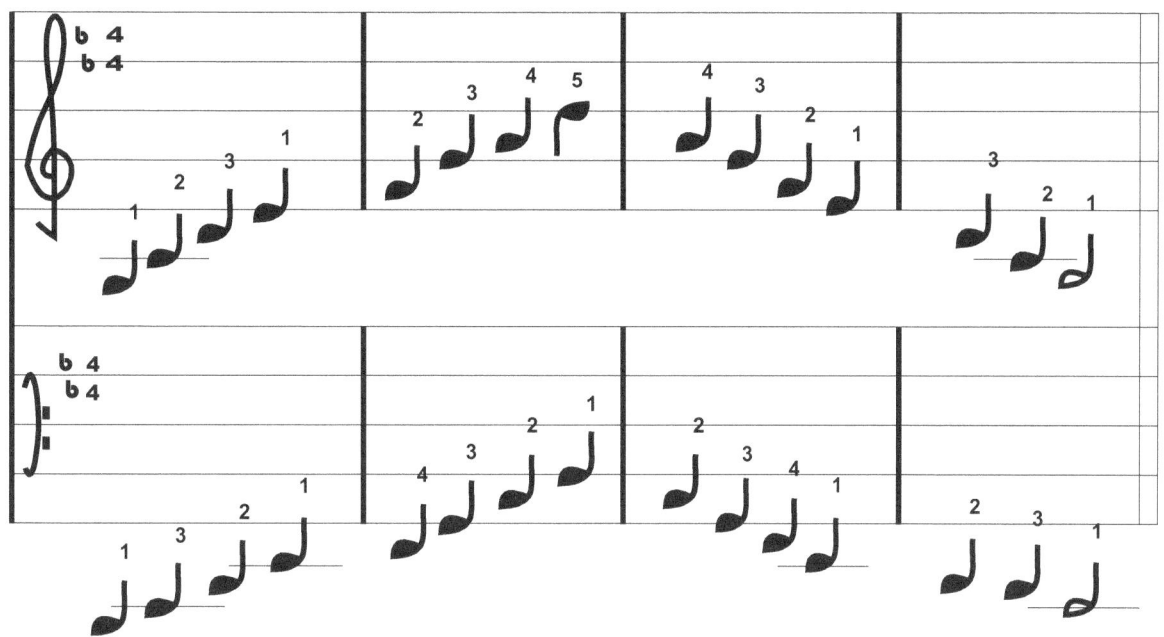

RIGHT HAND FINGERING OF MAJOR SCALE ON KEY **B**

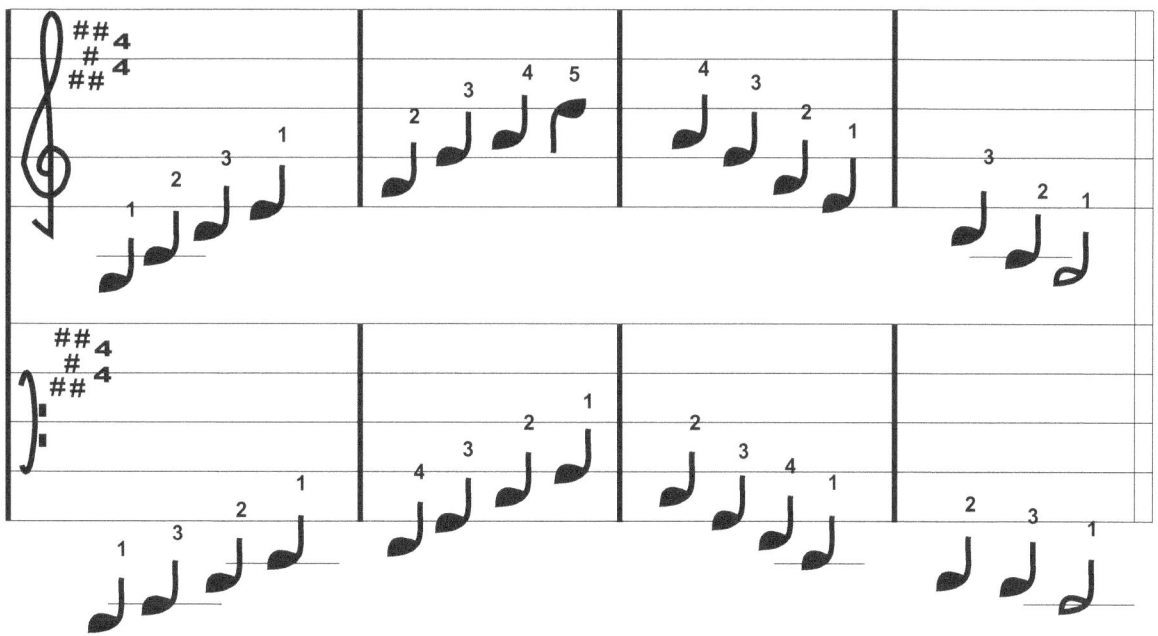

* The numbers on each musical note indicates the proper finger to use.

Play with the Right hand first, then Left hand, after mastering the proper fingering of the Major Scale on separate hands try and play the scale with both hands. .

SIMPLE TERMS AND ABBREVIATIONS IN MUSIC

Below are some of the musical terms and abbreviation used to tell how a musical piece should be played. It could be for a change of Key, Speed, Volume and style of music.

Musical Terms, Signs and Symbols

* Piano ----------------- Soft

* Mezzo Piano ------- Moderately soft

* Pianissimo ----------- Very soft

* Forte ----------------- Loud

* Mezzo forte --------- Moderately Loud

* Lento ----------------- Slow

* Largo ---------------- Slow and broad

* Poco a Poco ------- Little by little

* Presto --------------- Quick

* Prestissimo -------- As quick as possible

* Vivace -------------- Lively

* Bravo --------------- Great

* Gracioso ---------- Gracefully

* Fortissimo -------- Very loud

* Decrescendo ---- Gradually becoming softer

* Crescendo ------- Gradually becoming louder

* Allegro ------------- Fast

* Allegretto --------- Moderately fast

* Adagio ---------- Very slow

* Moderato ------ At a moderate pace

* Accelerando – Getting faster

* Rallentando — slowing down

* Ritenuto -------- Held back

* Legato ---------- Smoothly

* Marcia ---------- March

* Staccato ------- Short and distinct

* Ad libitum ----- At liberty

* Dal segno ------ Repeat from the sign

* Brillante --------- Brilliantly

PLAYING EXAMPLE SONGS ON STAVE

ELSHADDAI

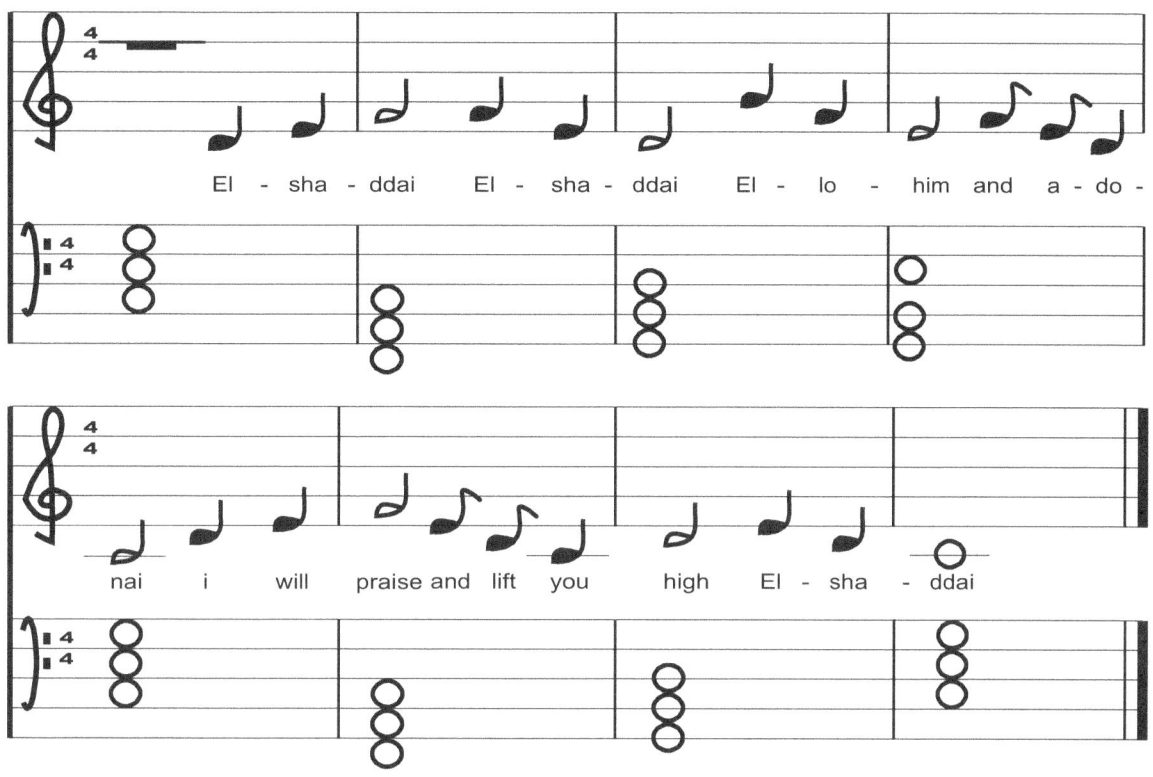

JEHOVAH YOU ARE THE MOST HIGH GOD

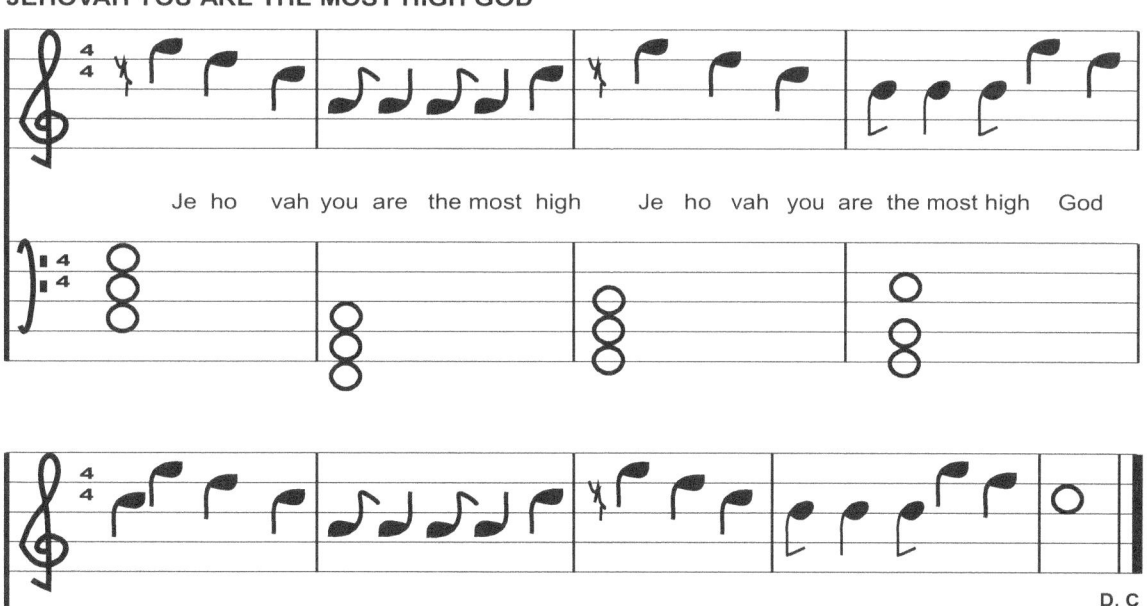

PLAYING EXAMPLE SONGS ON STAVE

MARY HAS A LITTLE LAMB

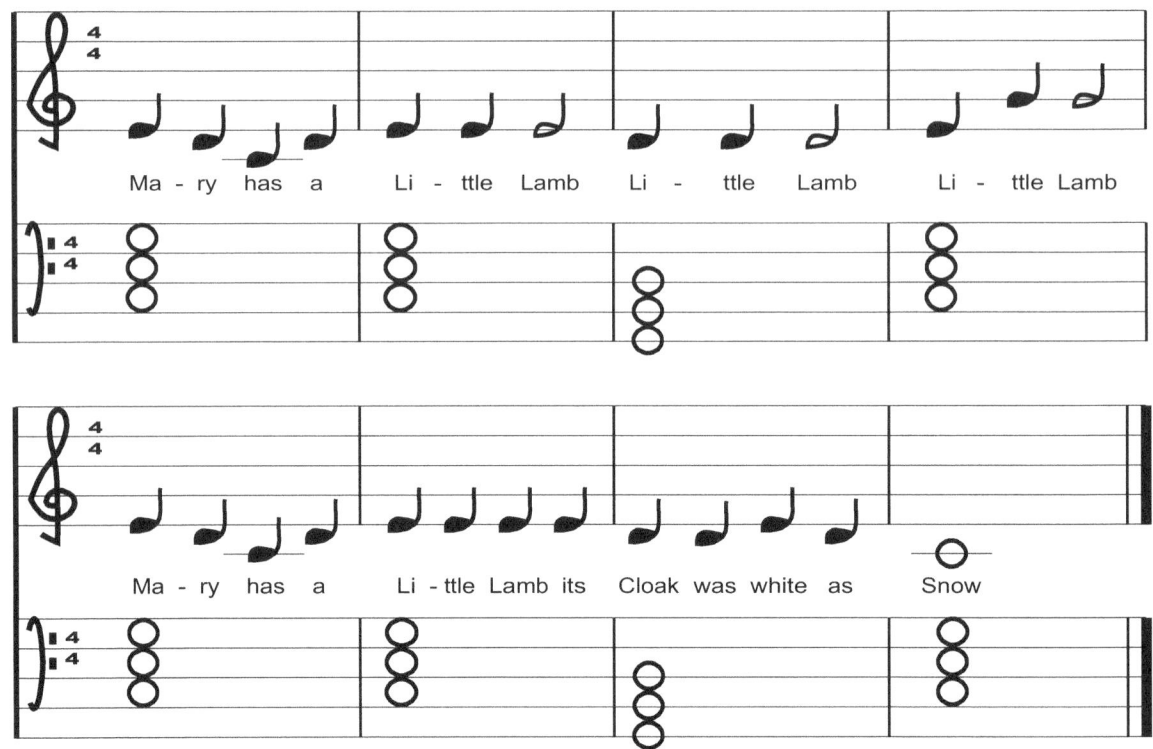

OUR GOD IS AWESOME

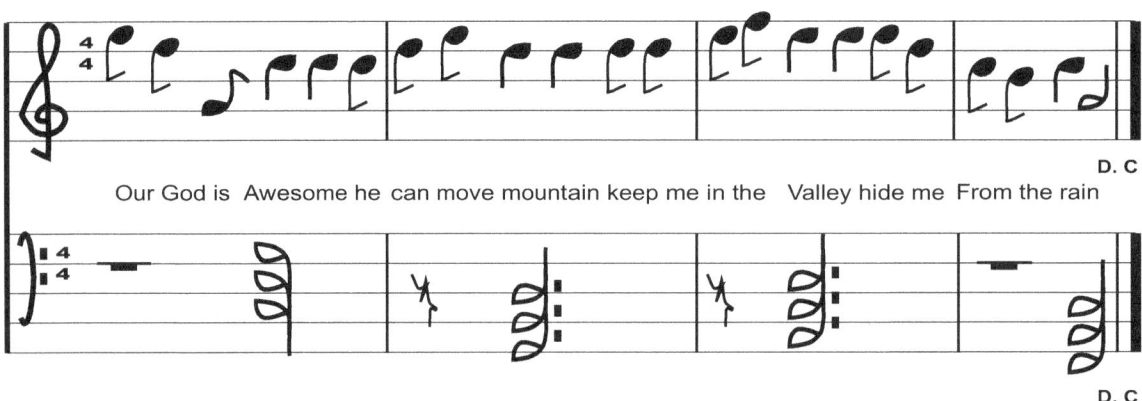

TWINKLE TWINKLE LITTLE STAR

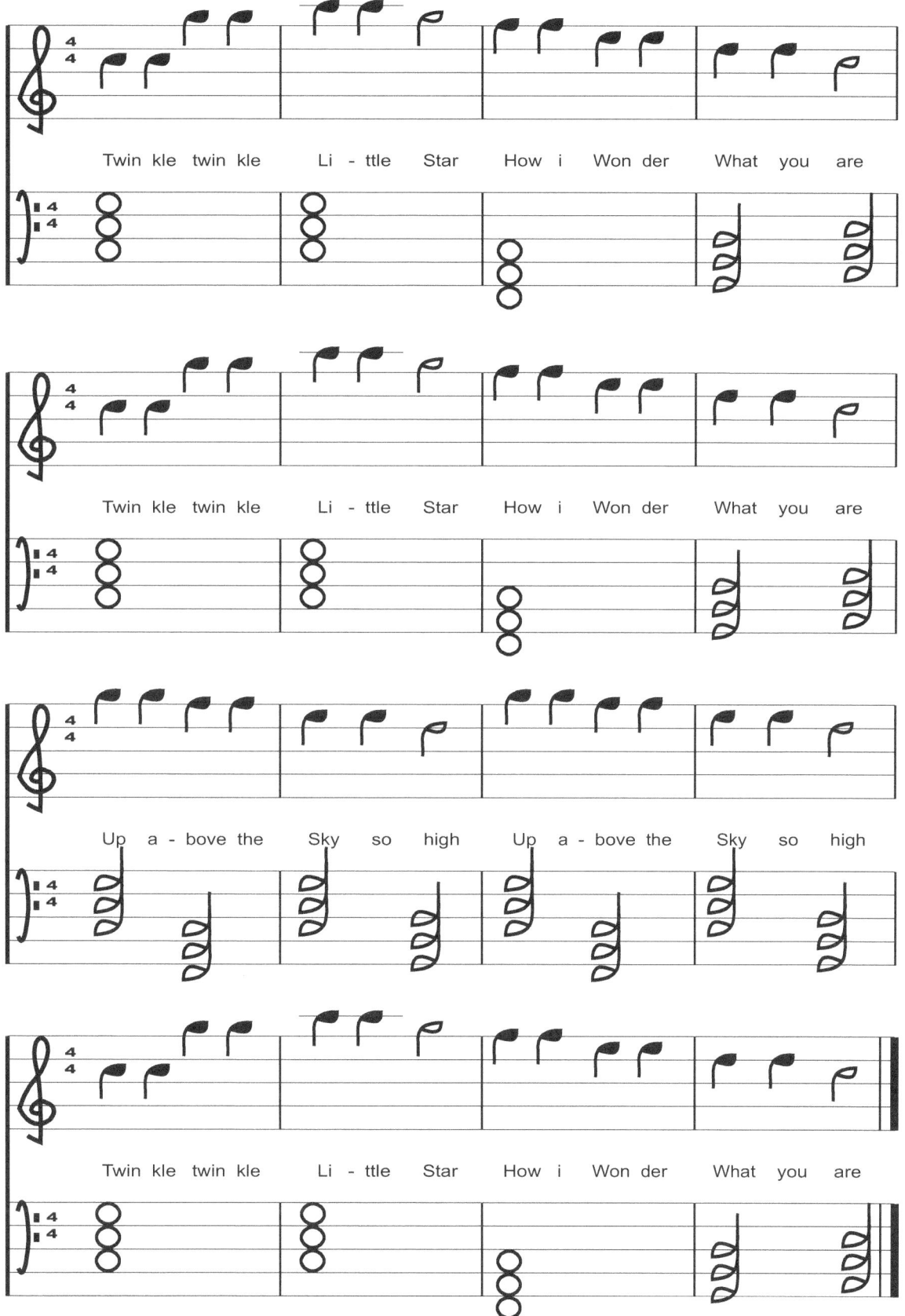

I NEED AN ANGEL

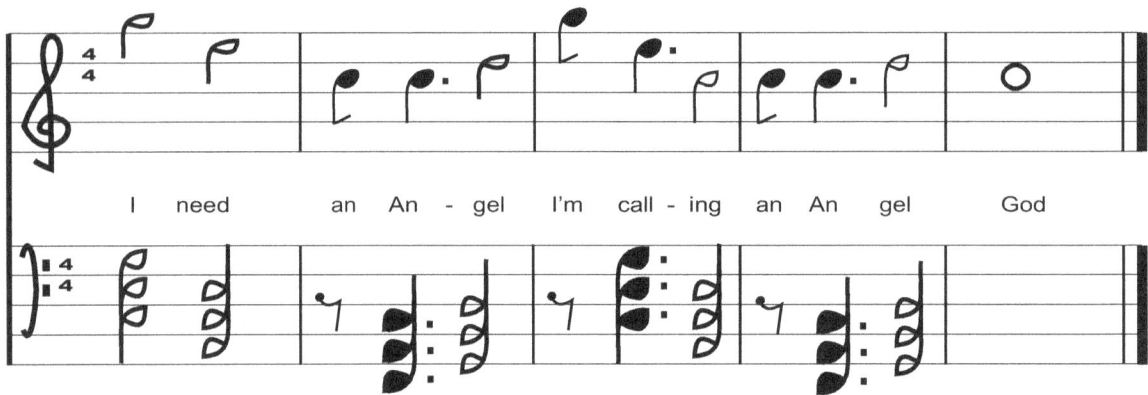

I need an An - gel I'm call - ing an An gel God

LONDON BRIDGE

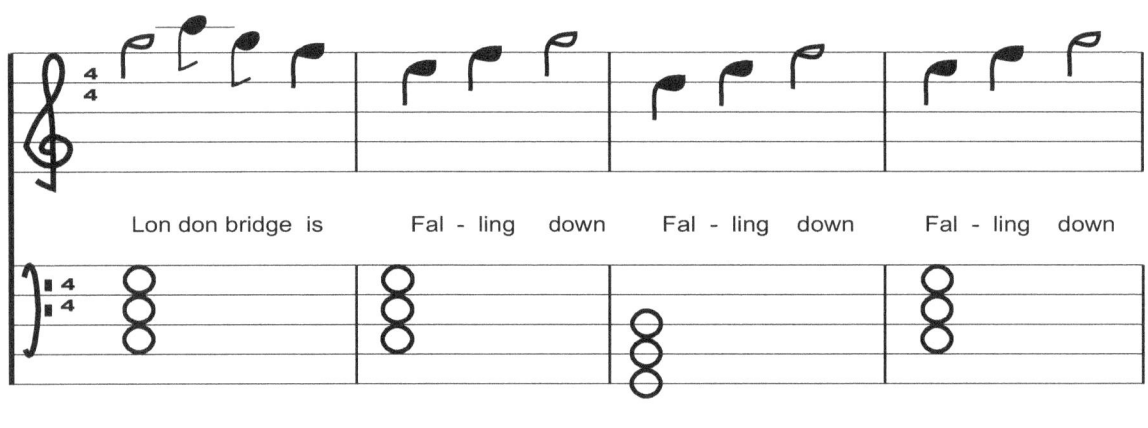

Lon don bridge is Fal - ling down Fal - ling down Fal - ling down

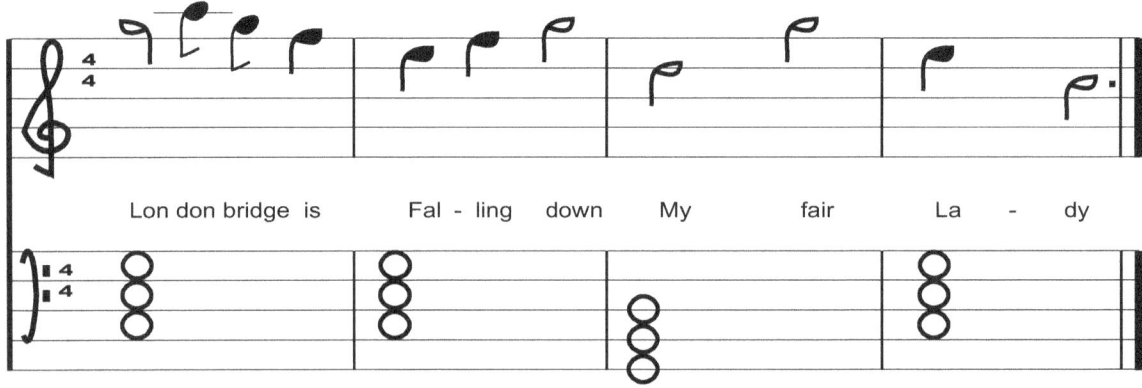

Lon don bridge is Fal - ling down My fair La - dy

JOY TO THE WORLD

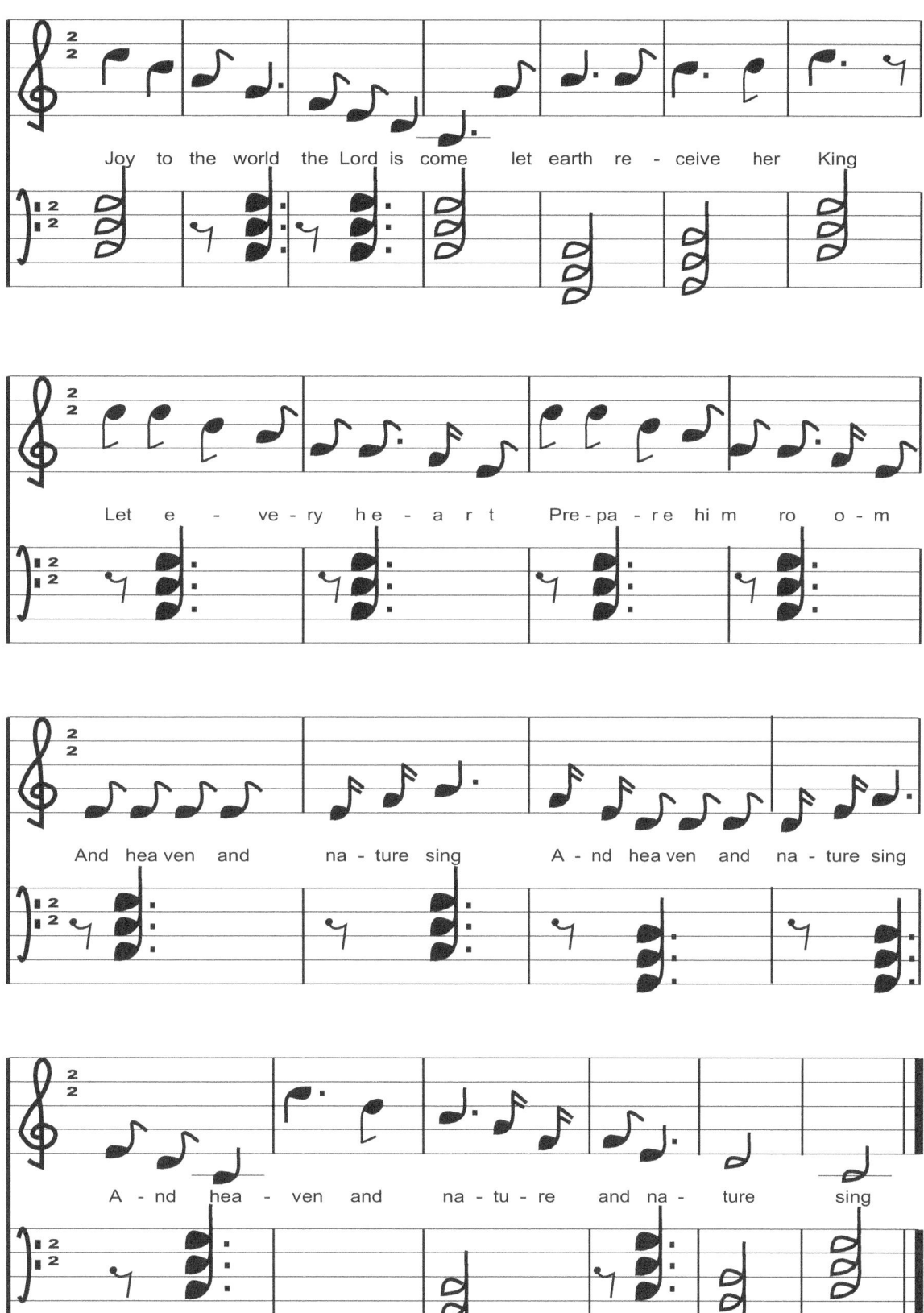

FELIZ NAVIDAD

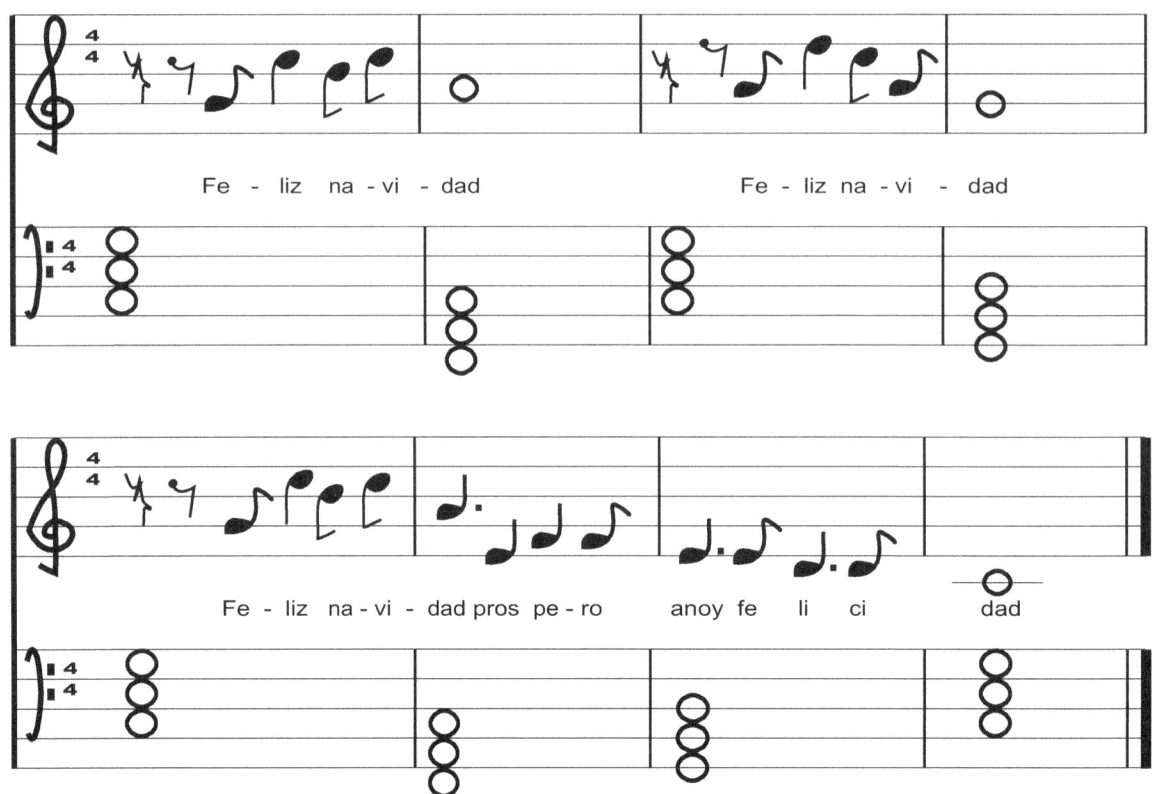

WE WANNA WISH YOU A-MERRY CHRISTMAS

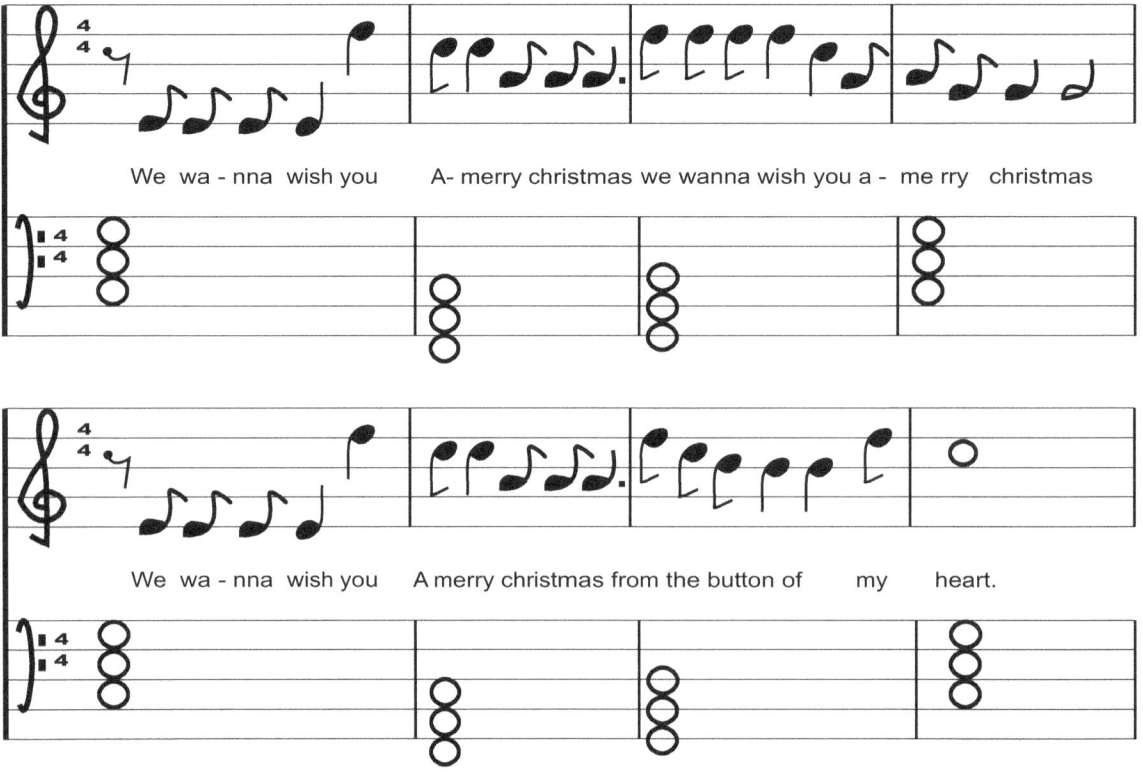

AUTUMN MARCH

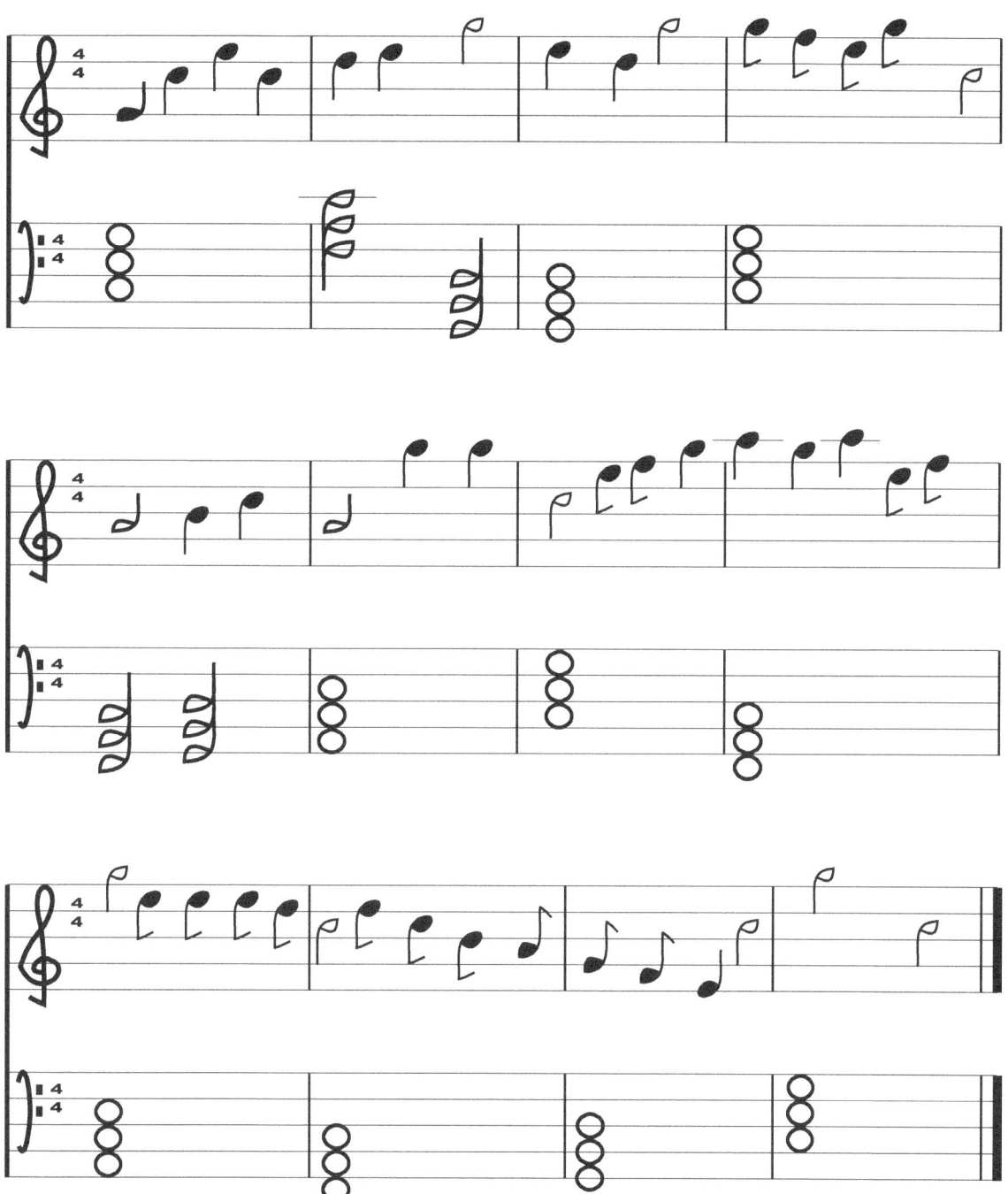

EVE DEW

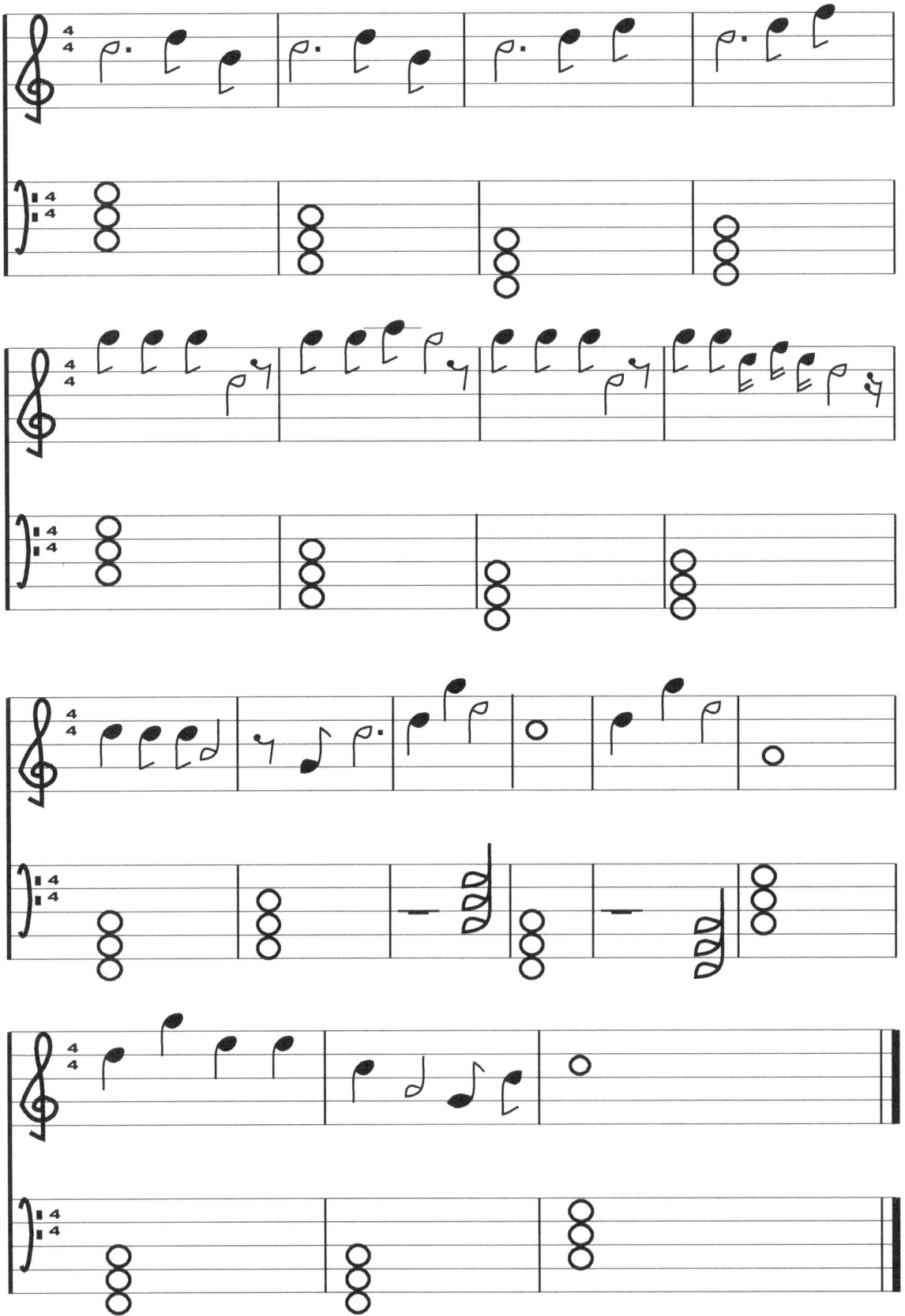

WHEN THE SAINTS GO MARCHING IN

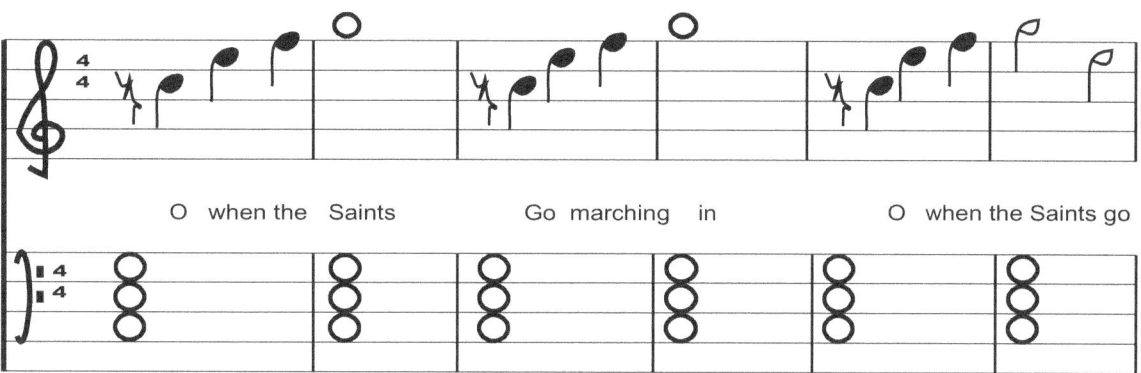

O   when the   Saints   Go   marching   in   O   when the Saints go

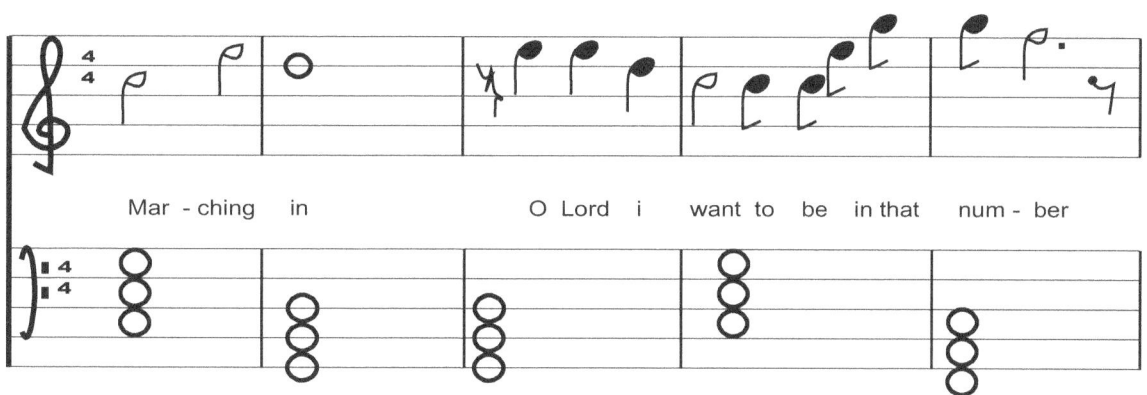

Mar - ching   in   O Lord i   want to be in that   num - ber

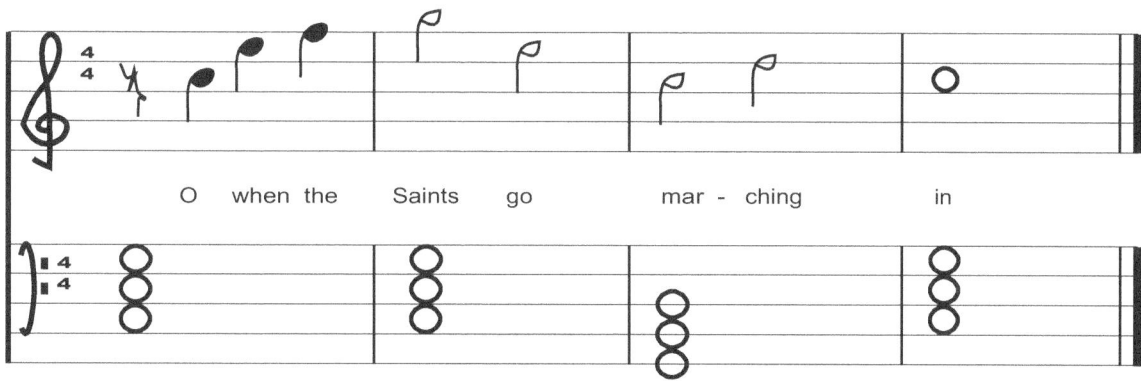

O   when the   Saints   go   mar - ching   in

I SURRENDER LORD

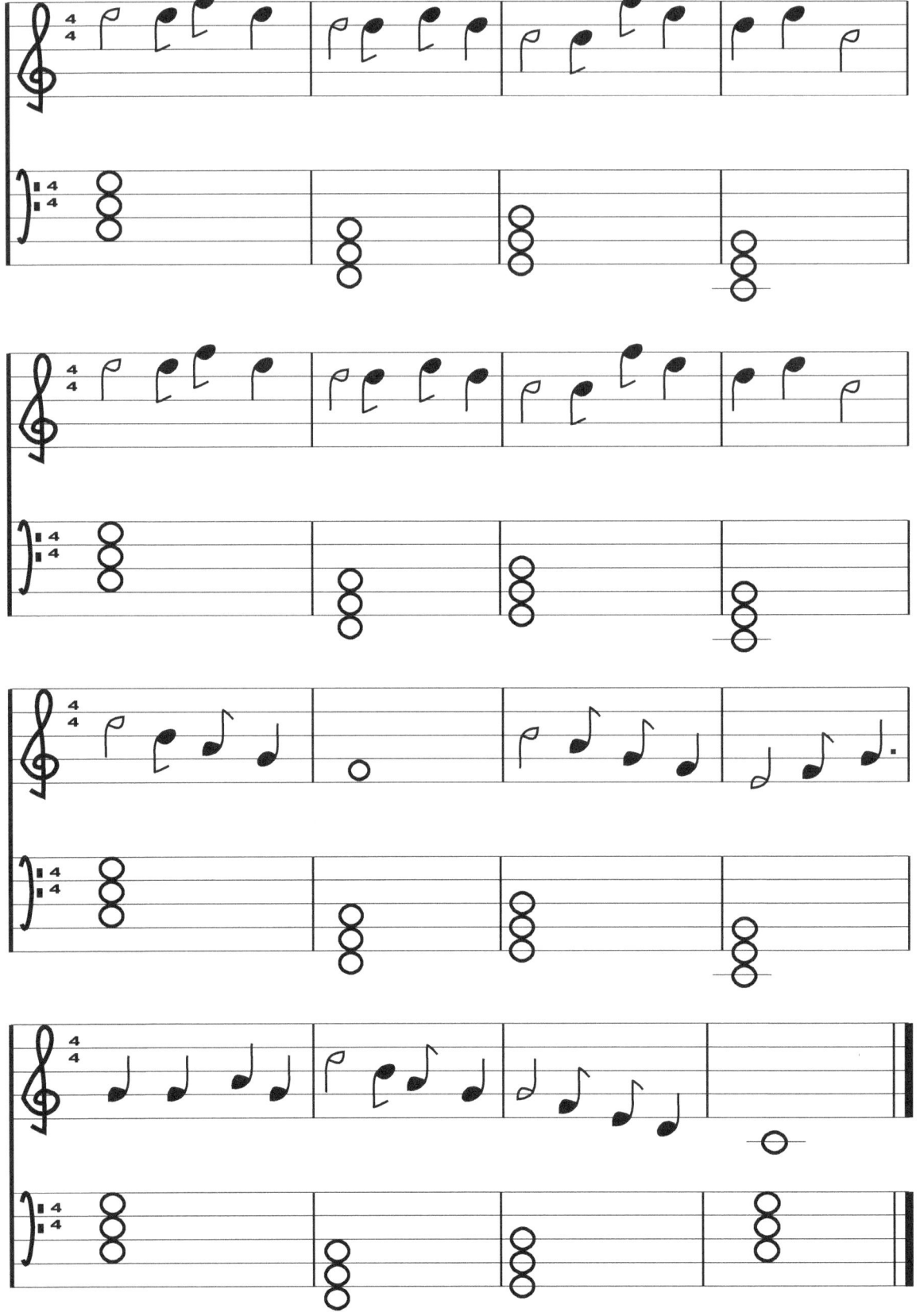

HAPPY BIRTHDAY

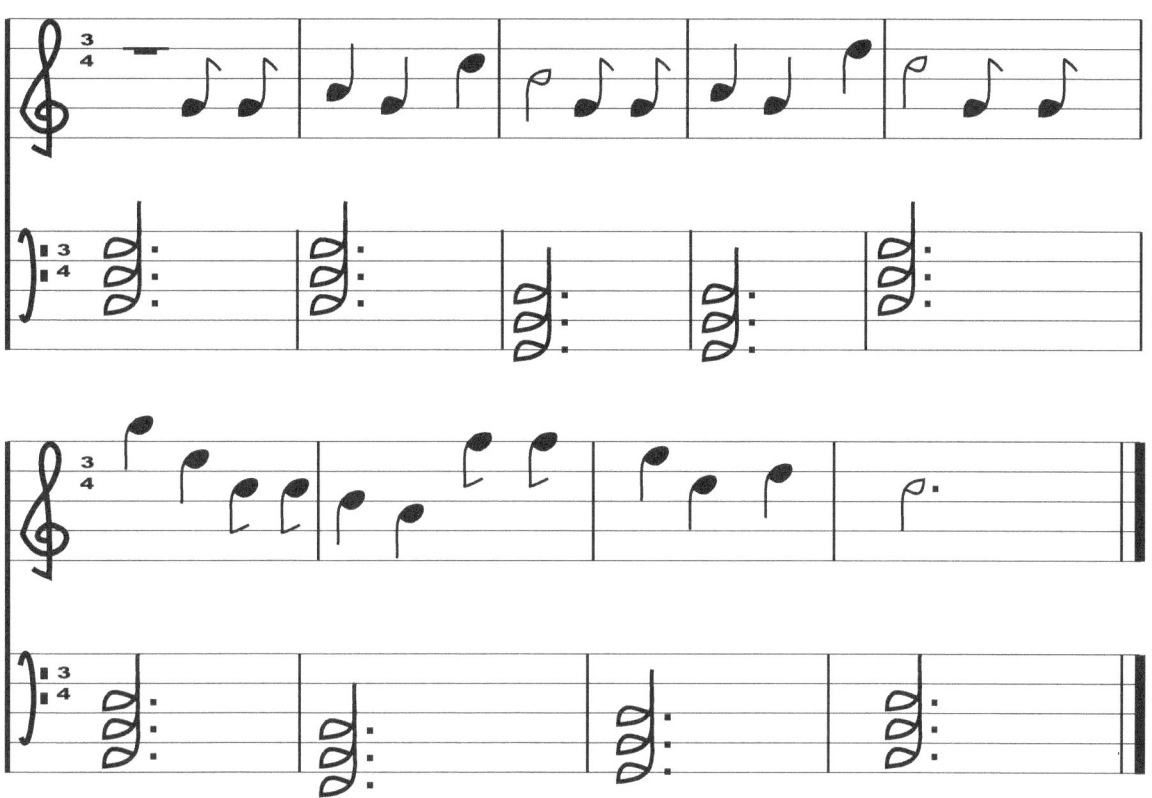

WE WISH YOU A MERRY CHRISTMAS

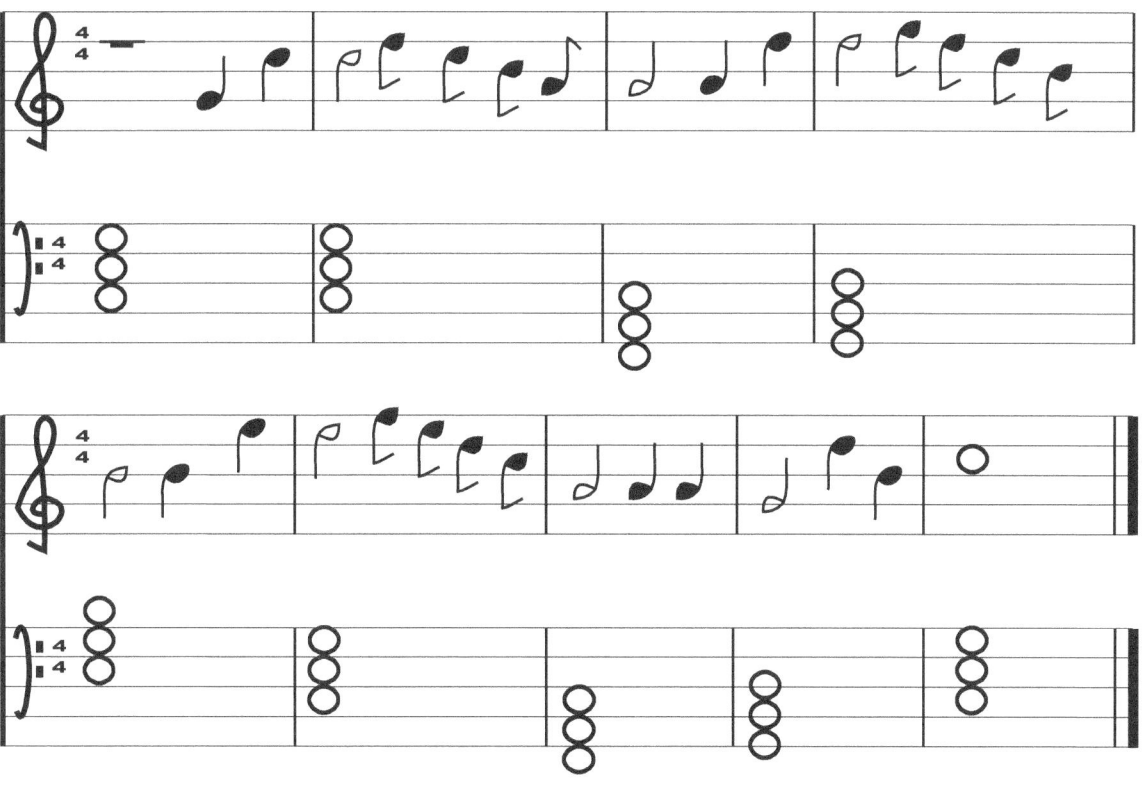

JINGLE BELL

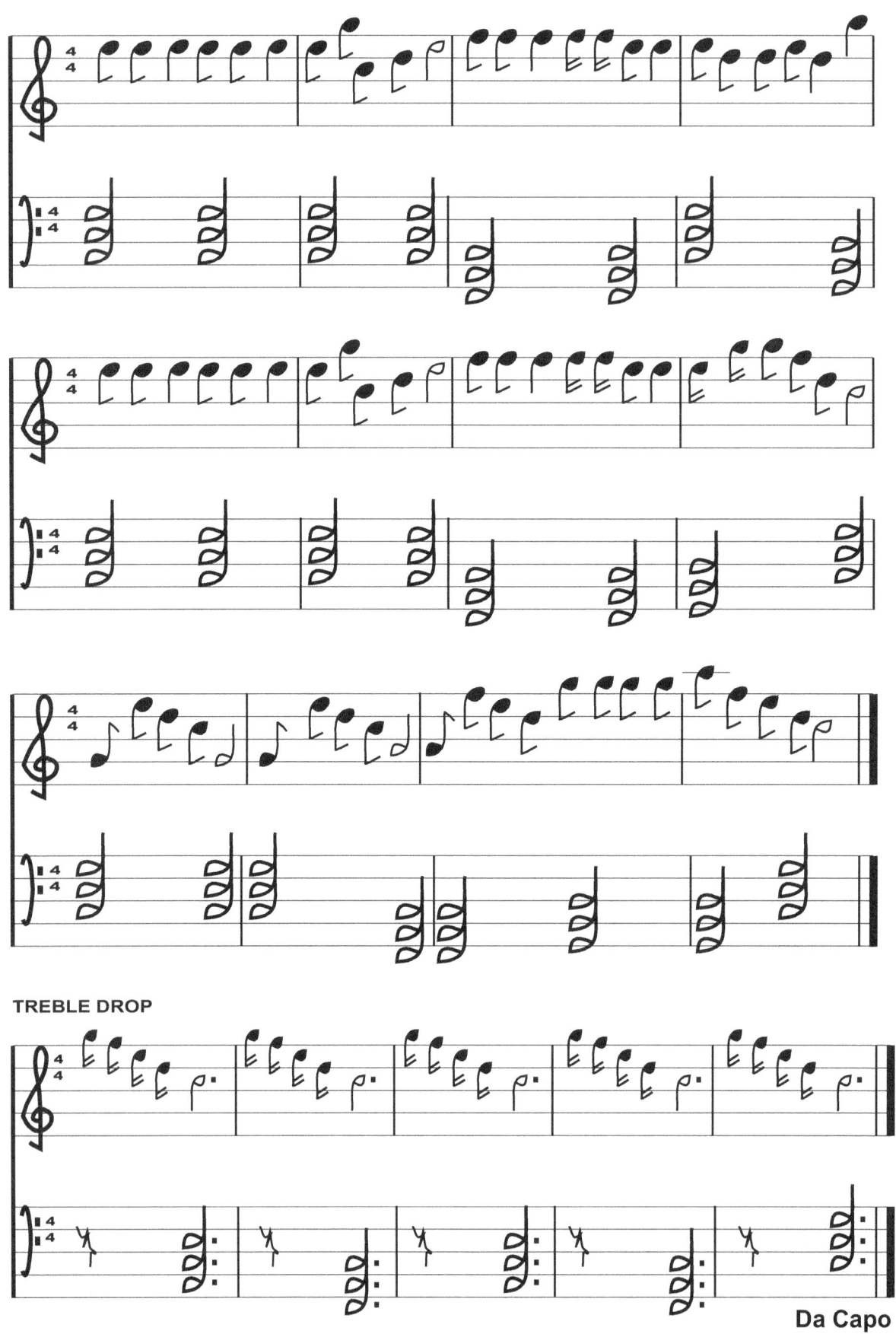

TREBLE DROP

Da Capo

Easy Way to Learn Piano and Sight Read

CANON

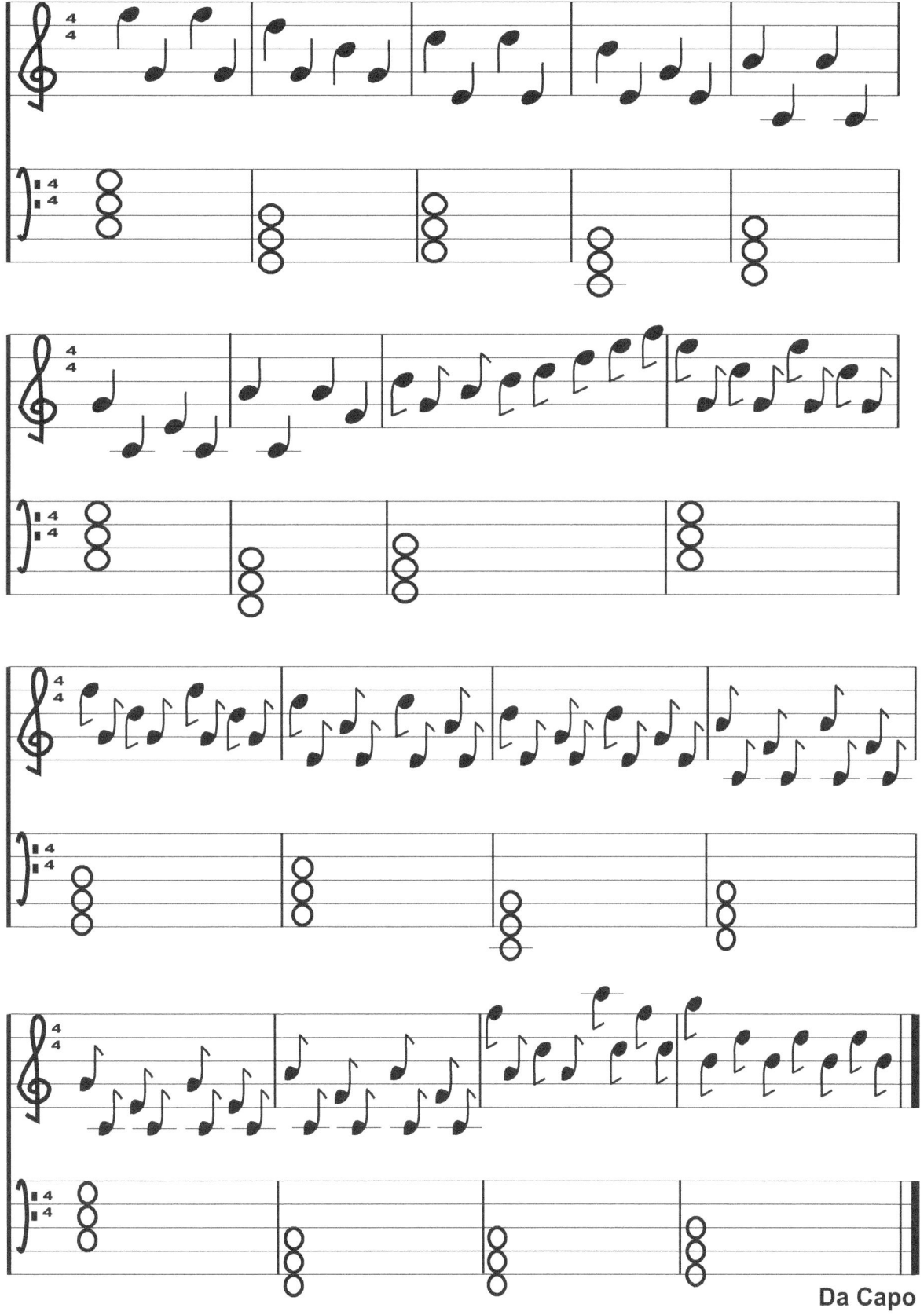

Da Capo

FUR ELISE

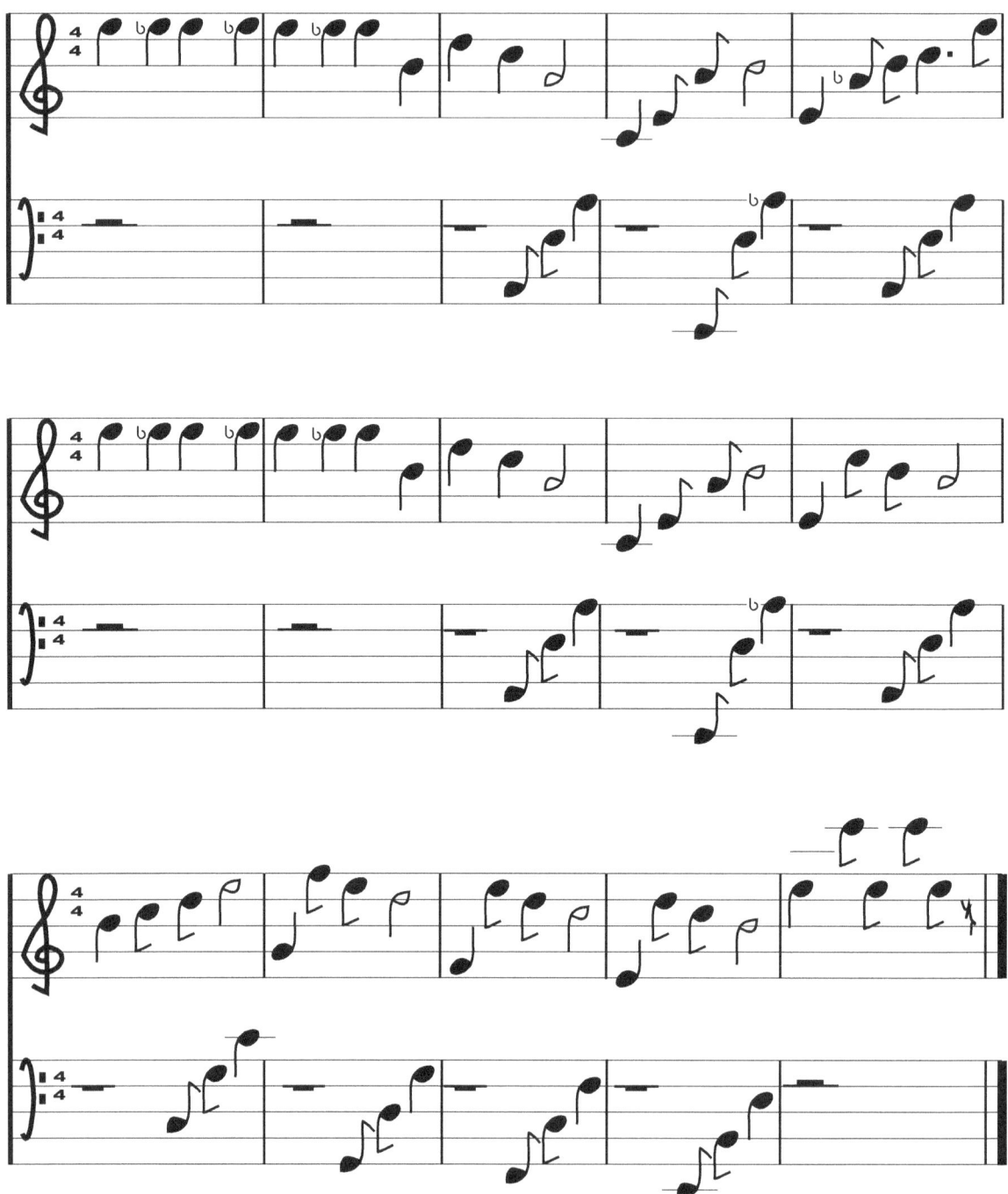

PERFECT SUS 2 MELODY

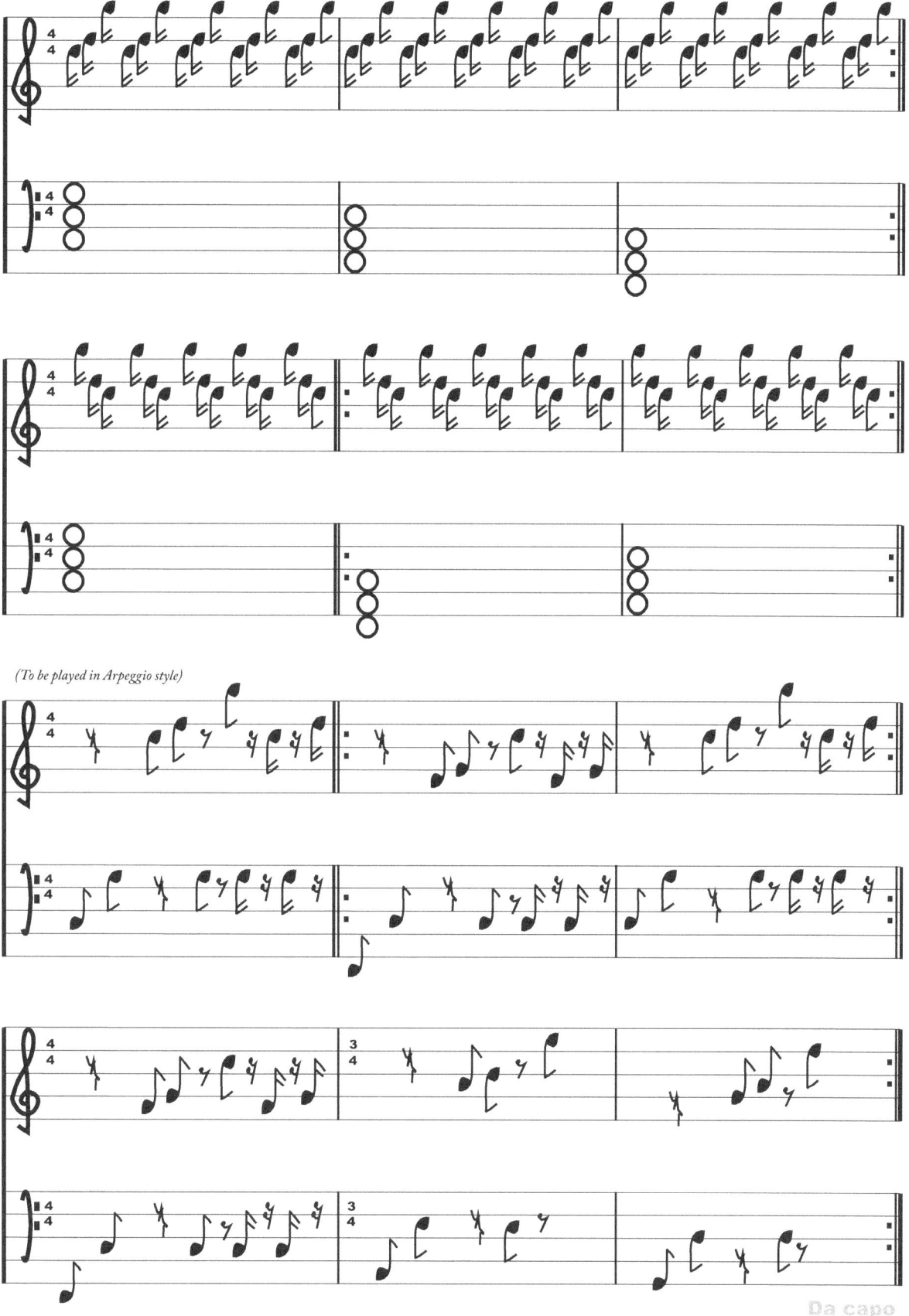

PENTATONIC SCALE

Scale Sol-fa notes: **do re mi so la do**

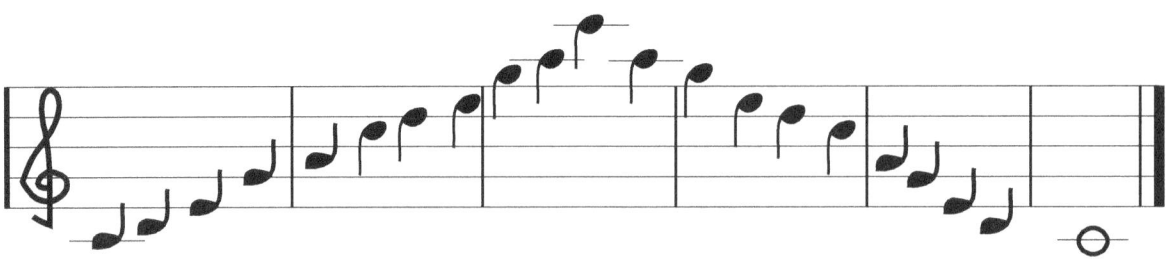

PENTATONIC MINOR SCALE

Scale Sol-fa notes: **do re mo so la do**

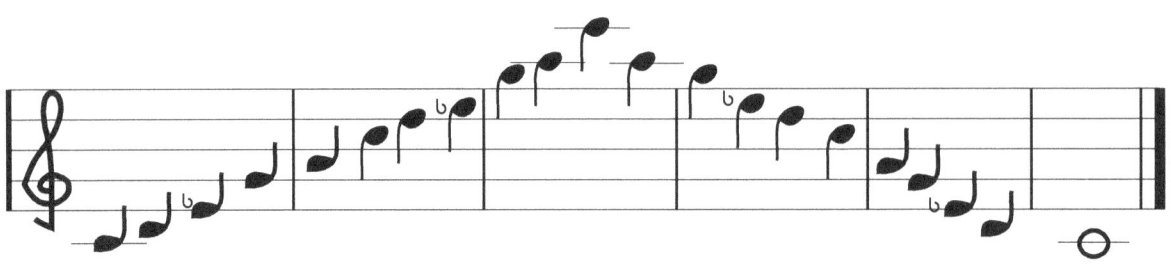

MAJOR BLUES SCALE
(Known as COUNTRY SCALE)

Scale Sol-fa notes: **do re mo mi so la do**

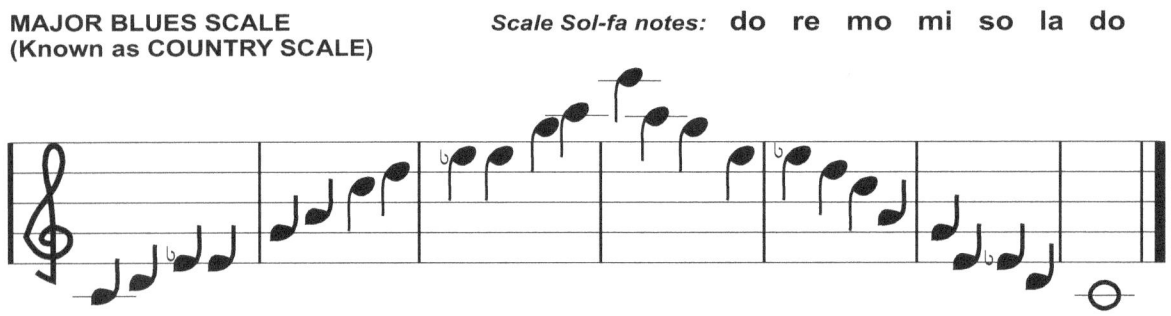

MINOR BLUES SCALE

Scale Sol-fa notes: **do mo fa fi so ta do**

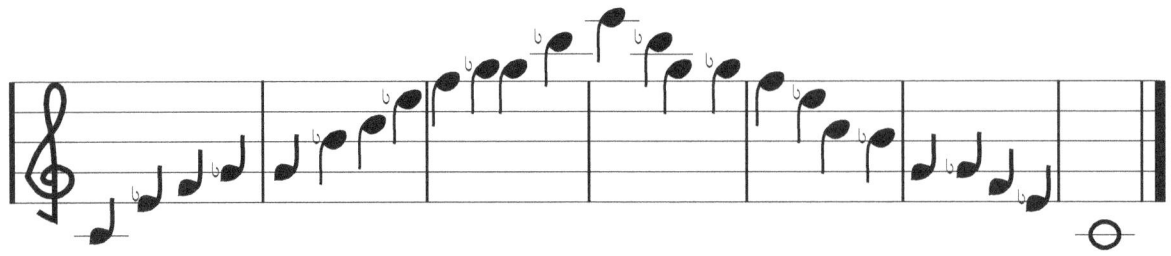

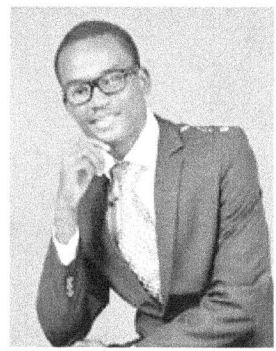

Hello my friend,

I'm Ezra Nwachukwu a Music Instructor, Designer and Writer. Thank you for buying a copy of this blessed musical book.

This book helps to build and develop one's knowledge in Music Rudiment, with Lots of practical Voice training Exercises and its Do's and Don't's. You'll be well informed and musically inclined as you take your time on each Exercise, Lesson and Examples to read and re-read, following the practical examples as shown.

I wish you success in your musical journey and Life in general.

Whatever your hand findeth to do, do it with all diligence,
"Seest thou a man diligent in his business? he shall stand before kings; he shall not stand before mean men. (Proverbs 22:29)"

Anything worth doing is worth doing well, and time to do that which makes you happy is a PRECIOUS GIFT, *(so Invest and make the best use of your time).*

As they say the Sky is your LIMIT.
The Optimistic thinkers say "The Sky is your *BEGINNING*".

But i say the Sky is your PLATFORM.

There is room enough for all the stars in the universe to shine freely, that's why they're ever shining come rain come sun!, There's no bitter competition among the Stars, they shine happily and brighter from their sphere.

It is an Awesome sight seeing many Stars shining together because their lights commensurate one another and they not only look beautiful together but they shine even brighter.

Your Stage Is Already Set in the Sky, I'm waiting to hear you,
Your friends are Waiting in Love to See you SHINE.

There's a great Potential within you.
BE GREAT.

Feel free to reach me via any of my contacts or social media to share Ideas, Feedbacks and I'll be glad to reply you as fast as I can, Thanks.

Telephone: +2348109845736

Email: Ezracreativeproductions@gmail.com

Website: EzraCreativeProductions.com

Your Humble Friend,
Ezra Nwachukwu
Best of Lucks.

www.ingramcontent.com/pod-product-compliance
Lightning Source LLC
Chambersburg PA
CBHW081053170526
45165CB00006B/2267